my

MY LIFE, MY WAY

how to make exceptional decisions about college, career, and life

ELYSE HUDACSKO

KDP

New York, New York

Thank you....

*To **my daughters** for inspiring me to write this book.*

May you lead the lives of your dreams!

*To **Lauren** and **Mary** for all of your thoughtful and useful feedback.*

Without you, this book would never have happened!

*To **Pascale** for being my accountability partner and friend through the writing of this book. (And for giving it a name!)*

Here's hoping we change the world!

*To **Marie** and **Suzanne** for all your faith, friendship, and encouragement.*

And the side-splitting laughter.

*And to **my husband** for tolerating seeing me only over my laptop screen for the better part of the year!*

Contents

Part V. Live an Exceptional Life

Part VI. And Now ...

INTRODUCTION

I am a reformed inadequate child.

A child who pushed her passions aside because they were not what she "should" do. A child who pursued talents that she did not enjoy because she "should" not waste them. A child who was told what success "should" look like.

I was the child who followed a life that well-meaning parents and teachers thought best for me.

And that conflicted with what set my soul on fire.

And that conflict shouted loudly to me each day "It is not okay to be yourself."

After years of exploration far out into the Universe and deep down inside myself, I have found what sets my soul on fire and I have transformed my life from mediocre to exceptional.

A life where I get to be my authentic self every day.

I want to guide you to have this kind of exceptional life.

PART I

WHAT KIND OF LIFE DO YOU WANT?

I bet that if you could have any life you wanted, you would pick a joyful, exceptional life. A life filled with amazing experiences that help you to grow and allow you to share the very best of yourself with others.

1.

You Need Help. You Really Do.

"The mass of men lead lives of quiet desperation."

- Henry David Thoreau (transcendentalist)

A Long, Long Time Ago in A Galaxy ...

... a few miles from New York City lived a young girl preparing to set off on her own. She had near perfect SAT scores. She loved to dance. She loved her Rolodex (like Contacts on your phone... except they're on little paper cards). She loved sneaking out at lunch for the perfect hamburger at the grill across the street. She was great at math. She liked boys. A lot. She went to parties. And she had no idea what she wanted to do with her life.

She made it to Cornell University (you know, an Ivy League school, practically the first cousin of Harvard or Yale) and spent four years taking classes, joining a sorority, going to parties, dating more boys, working at a cushy on-campus job, avoiding the dining hall in favor of pizza and cookie delivery. It was all okay. But this life didn't really light her up. Because still, she just didn't know what she wanted her life to look like.

She got a job with a Fortune 500 company and moved to New York City. She commuted to Wall Street each day in super cute shoes. She had Sunday brunch on the Upper East Side every weekend. She went to concerts in the park. She shopped at Tiffany's. She married a guy. She went on fabulous vacations. To most, her life looked perfect – she had achieved the glitzy NY twenty-something dream. But on the inside, there wasn't even a tiny sparkle. Because she still wasn't living the life of HER dreams.

In case you haven't already guessed, this girl is me. And thankfully, after almost two decades, I figured out how to live a joyful, exceptional life! I stopped living the life that was expected of me. I figured out who I was and what lit my soul on fire. I learned how to follow a path that allows me to have the experiences that I want, helps me to grow, and allows me to share my gifts with the world. And I discovered some life-changing practices that keep my life flowing peacefully in the direction I desire.

And I am here to share it all with you.

You Have Some Decisions to Make. And Some Choices.

You are at a point in your life where you are probably making decisions about college or career. But you also have an important choice. You can choose to know yourself and what lights you up inside and use that knowledge to live a joyful, exceptional life. Or you can choose to make your decisions based on what everyone else is doing or what others are telling you that you should do.

I want to help you choose to live a joyful life.
Let me show you how we (yes, we) are going to do it.

Let Me Tell You About the Journey We Are Going to Take... Together

Don't think of this as a book, think of it as your guide. It is not only for you to read. It is to help you explore and to discover the greatest single thing in this universe ... you!

There are lots of exercises to help you get to know yourself better, set your direction, and live an exceptional life. Some exercises require you to do some journaling, some are artistic, some require interaction, some are field trips. (You know you love field trips!)

To help you along you will need a journal. You can use a fancy journal or a plain spiral-bound notebook or a document on your laptop.

And there are also lots of stories. Many about me and my adventures. I will share the good, the bad... and the laughable (don't judge!). But there are also lots of stories about other people who have taken similar routes. And some about people who have been living exceptional lives since they were barely out of diapers.

During our time together you are going to rediscover your passion, clarify your talent, figure out how you want to impact this world, define success, and find your happy places. You are going to learn how they all combine together in a balanced way as your authentic self. You are going to develop a unique direction for your life that allows you to celebrate your authentic, truest self. And you are going to learn to live an exceptional life by discovering how to navigate yourself through this great Universe.

Note: Your real work begins in Part 3 and you can feel free to skip ahead and get started. In Part 2, I help you to embrace the idea that you are allowed to want and have an exceptional life. So I really encourage you to read straight through to build a solid foundation for the work you are going to do, especially if you are at all concerned that an exceptional is something everyone can have.

So, let's get started.
But first... a word of caution.

Content with A Mediocre Life? Then This Book Isn't for You.

This book is not for everybody.

This book is not for those of you who are willing to live a life lacking in joy in exchange for safety and security. This book is not for those of you who are happy doing what everyone else is doing. This book is not for those of you who want someone else to tell you what to do. This book is not for those of you who think that joy is simply a luxury item. This book is not for those of you who are content with mediocre.

This book is for those of you out there who are longing for something more, for those of you who want to live a life full of moments that you love. This book is a love letter to those of you who believe that every moment of your journey is important and deserves to be exceptional. This book is for those of you who are willing to do some deep work getting to know yourself. This book is for those of you who are ready to embrace a new way of thinking and are willing to try some new practices in living. This book is for those of you who accept that failures and challenges are part of growth. This book is for those of you who have the courage and perseverance to follow what you know instead of what you are told. This book is for those of you who want to live an exceptional life. In every single moment.

If you have gotten this far, I think you are ready for this quest to exceptional.

Now that you're ready for your journey to the life you deserve, I can't wait to show you what it can look like.

2.

An Exceptional Life Comes from Living Your Own Truth

"We have to dare to be ourselves, however frightening or strange that self may prove to be."

- May Sarton (poet and novelist)

What Do I Mean By "Exceptional Life"?

Since the whole point of this book is to help you to live an exceptional life, let's talk about what that looks like.

For me, it is spending hours each day learning by reading, listening to podcasts, and talking with people about self-development and education. It is sharing what I learned with others through homeschooling my kids, writing books (like this one), running workshops for young adults looking for direction, and working on blog posts for people who know there is something more to life. I love that I get to do hours of research and organize everything I have learned to help spark positive transformation in others! I also love trying new recipes (I am now a master at pita bread!), holing myself up to work on crafts (I learned how to knit on a loom), taking dance classes (I've learned to belly dance), and dabbling in art (check out @mudandmoon on Instagram to see some of my work). I also love waking up early and having a few hours of quiet time before the rest of the house gets up. I travel and try new restaurants often. I walk and practice yoga every day. I get to see a few Broadway shows every year. This is what my exceptional life looks like.

And guess what? That probably sounds pretty terrible to more than a few of you!

That's because an exceptional life is a life that allows you to spend each day doing what brings YOU great joy. An exceptional life comes from knowing what lights you up inside and agreeing to live in a way that allows the light to grow and flourish. It is a life full of experiences that you love. It is about loving what you are doing so much that you want to learn as much as you can about it and you want to share it with anyone who will listen!

Living an exceptional life means living a life doing the things that bring YOU joy. And that means ignoring the things other people think you "should" be doing (if they don't bring you joy!). It is about looking at each opportunity that comes along and deciding if it will make you happy and passing on the things that won't. Taking time for you, not being bullied or shamed into doing things that don't feel right, embracing your uniqueness. That is a joyful, exceptional life.

Please note, a mediocre life is one filled with other people's priorities. A life filled with things that you feel like you have to do but don't want to do. A job you aren't passionate about. Investing your time in things you don't care about. Believing that taking time for yourself is selfish.

An exceptional life is a life that makes you want to jump out of bed each morning. And it's something you can learn to have.

Together we are going to discover what makes you jump.

How You Get to An Exceptional Life

This book is going to guide you along the path to an exceptional life. (As long as you do the work!)

First, you are going to discover your authentic self. You might think you know yourself. And you probably do. On the surface. But you have probably not spent much time alone with yourself asking yourself what really lights you up inside. We are going to do that. Together. You are going to remember your passion. You are going to get clear on your talents. You are going to think about how you want to impact the world. You are going to think about success in a whole new way. And you are going to identify exactly what you need to be happy. When you put this all together you are going to know what makes you glow. You are going to know your authentic self.

Next, you are going to learn to follow the direction of your authentic self. Your own unique direction. I am going to help you embrace every moment of this journey of life and make fearless choices. I am going to help you get comfortable with all of the changes the Universe throws at you. I am going to help you see that education is much broader and deeper than just the school you pick and that career in can be thought about in a whole new way. And I am going to help you tackle the voice inside (and out) that screams that you can't follow your dreams. You are going to develop a direction that is uniquely yours and that is aligned with your authentic self.

Then I am going to share some practices with you that have allowed me to follow my own unique direction with grace and peace.

I am going to inspire you to make fearless choices and handle what the world throws at you. I am going to show you a different way to look at the ladder of success. I am going to teach you to embrace gratitude as an integral part of your life. We are going to touch on using your intuition and manifesting your dreams. And I am going to encourage you to build a support network to help you keep following your true north.

When we are done with this adventure, you will know so much more about yourself and will be well equipped to live an exceptional life.

It may sound like a dream, but I promise, it is real!

It Really Does Exist!

To inspire you just a bit, I want to tell you about a young woman who is living an exceptional life.

I have known Diana since she was a little girl wearing frilly dresses and I have watched her grow into not only a lovely young woman, but into a person who is living an exceptional life every day. I get a little teary every time I think about her!

Diana is an accomplished youth folk singer whose original music is being played on radio stations all across the country. She travels the country opening for popular bands and shares her gift of song at theaters, cafes, retreats, and conferences. Diana writes her music, not because she wants to be a famous musician (I mean, she does, but that's not her motivation), but because she is putting to paper what she feels in her heart. Her songs are beautiful and really enjoyable to listen to. Her songs tell the stories of her life and are inspiring to others. Every day she is living an exceptional life by spending time doing what she loves and sharing it with others.

When you look at Diana, it is crystal clear that she is living a life aligned with her authentic self.

As a kid, there was one thing Diana really loved. Singing. It was her passion.

I remember asking her once when she started singing and before she could answer her younger brother jumped in and said, "When was she ever not singing?" He told me that when they were in the car listening to music he could never hear the song because Diana was always singing along. Her mother chimed in that if she wasn't singing she was at least humming!

And now Diana gets to sing all day, every day.

But, an exceptional life is not just about passion. It is also about bringing your talents to your passion. And Diana has been able to do just that.

Two of the talents that I recognized in Diana, and that she has incorporated into her lifestyle, are her ability to communicate with maturity and enthusiasm and her love of kids. In these, areas, she always impressed me.

I have to admit that before I had my own children, I was a little afraid of kids. I never knew what to talk about or how to respond to what they told me! But every time Diana and I were in the same place, I always found myself trying to pair off with her to get the scoop on her life in her bubbly, confident, funny way. I loved listening to her. She spoke with such authenticity and confidence. She drew you into her story and made you want to hear more.

And I loved watching her with kids. When Diana was a younger teen her family moved away, and we would visit once a year. By this time, I had kids of my own (and they of course came along for the visit). I can remember each time we arrived she (and her equally amazing brother) swept those kids out of the car the minute we hit the driveway and took them on tours of the house or out to play with the dogs. Within fifteen minutes she had them at the pool or in the car headed for ice cream. She was the first person I ever let babysit them! Diana had a real gift for relating to kids. To this day, my kids are utterly enthralled with her.

Diana has taken these talents and applied them to her music. Her understanding of young people and her ability to communicate with honesty and excitement, make her music accessible and inspiring to today's kids. And not only is she singing to them, she speaks to them as well. Diana is bringing her music to an exceptional level by combining her talent with her passion.

Diana has made sure that her musical career allows her to do the things that make her happy. She travels a ton, spends lots of time with her family, and is never too far from a dog. She is not willing to sacrifice her happiness, she is only willing to make it a part of her everyday life.

Diana refuses to compromise on the lyrics of her music. She wants to make a difference to today's youth and will not sing songs that won't allow her to do that. She insists that her songs mean something.

Diana is clear on what makes her feel successful. Creating a powerful message is more important than money. Kindness is more important than fame. Honesty is more important than brand. Diana measures herself only by her own standards, not someone else's.

Diana knows what kind of life she wants to have. A life aligned with her passion and talents and her ideas about happiness, impact, and success. And it is pretty clear that she is living it.

Now you may ask, "Who gave Diana this exceptional life?"

Who Is Responsible for Giving You an Exceptional Life?

You are responsible for your life. Nobody is going to hand it to you. You are the only person who can choose to live a joyful, exceptional life. You are the one who can choose an exceptional life by taking control over the decisions in your life. You are the one who can take responsibility for your actions and creations and plans.

Nobody handed Diana or me our exceptional lives. We created them for ourselves. We did the work to know what lit us up inside by digging deep and listening. We chose to follow paths that aligned with the authentic selves we discovered and allowed our lives to be guided by practices we believed in.

We created our own exceptional lives. Just like you are going to do.

You get to choose what kind of life you want.
Choose exceptional. I'm here to help.

PART II

THE UN-TRUTHS WE HAVE BEEN TOLD

Before we get started down your path to an exceptional life, I want to talk about a few of the reasons most people are not living joyful, exceptional lives.

3.

"You Don't Know What You Want"

"If you are not excited about it, it's not the right path."

– Esther Hicks (inspirational speaker)

A lot of people think that when you are young, you can't possibly know what you want. So many people buy into this and wait until their lives are half over to get to know themselves.

I don't agree.

The Biggest Mistake

What is the biggest mistake you can make, you ask? Picking the wrong major? Forgetting deodorant? Kissing your best friend's girlfriend? All bad. (Well, maybe the deodorant thing is really bad.) But not the biggest mistake you can make.

The biggest mistake you can make is buying into the idea that you are too young to know what you want. Not investing the time to get to know who you are. Or knowing who you are and discarding it.

When you don't know who you are and what you want, you end up letting others (e.g. parents, teachers, friends, society) set your life direction for you. The only way to live the life of your dreams is to figure out the direction for yourself and then head in that direction every single day. Taking little baby steps and the occasional giant leap.

Think of it like this. It's like going out for ice cream and not realizing that you want a banana split with rocky road ice cream and caramel sauce. Instead, you let someone else order for you, and that single scoop of strawberry ice cream leaves you feeling sadly unfulfilled.

It seems like a no-brainer, but a lot of people make this mistake. Including me.

That Big Mistake? I Made It.

For years I had no idea who I was or what I wanted. I made choices about college and career based on what other people told me was good for me. What other people told me I could and couldn't have. What made other people happy. And I was mediocre at all I did, both in what I provided to others and my own joy in life, because I was living a life that was not of my own choosing.

When I was where you are or may be now, I had no idea who I was or the direction I wanted to follow. It had been lost. Erased when I was little. I followed my parents and teachers desire that I study engineering because I was so good at math (and a girl, to boot!) and got a job as a computer programmer.

These were not my dreams, they belonged to someone else. I got no joy from the physics, calculus and computer courses I studied in college. I had a dismal 2.8 GPA and barely graduated because for four years I sat in huge lecture halls listening to professors talk about things that I could have cared less about. I could not make heads or tails of what I was meant to be learning because I wasn't at all interested in how machines were built or programmed. I got even less joy from my job writing programs for an investment bank. I had zero interest in financial services and even less in COBOL (that is a really old programming language that I really hope nobody uses anymore!).

Now, don't get me wrong, I had a "good" life. A decent salary. Friends. Great shoes. A nice apartment. Parties every weekend. A vacation every year. But in reality, all that did not make up for living a bland existence for 90% of my waking hours.

In my thirties I got a wakeup call and realized I wanted more out of life. The tragedy of September 11th happened. There was so much loss around me in New York. Employees of my company, kids from my hometown, a boy I had a crush on. I returned to work in a daze a few days later. Heartbroken like everyone else. But on that day, I got word that an old friend had died on one of the top floors of the North Tower. I cried my eyes out as I remembered his beautiful soul. His name was Peter and he lived upstairs from me. Every night I could hear the whine of his Ducati motorcycle as he pulled in front of the building. I would grab two glasses of wine and he would meet me on the roof with his favorite cigar. We would talk about work and weekends and the meaning of life. He was always full of questions about my hopes and dreams and favorite TV show and full of insights about love and family and cooking the perfect fried egg.

Peter loved life. He was passionate about his job in banking. He could go on for an hour in excited tones about something that happened that day. About someone he helped or something he created. But he was always home by seven each night because life was not all about work for him. He rode his motorcycle the hundred or so blocks to and from work in custom suits that he loved. He loved reading the classics and cooking fabulous meals and Sunday brunch. He lived a life that made him excited to get out of bed each day.

A few days after September 11th, as I sat at my desk remembering these wonderful things about Peter, the managing partner of our company ran past my office calmly explaining that there had been another bomb threat. There were many after September 11th in New York City. I left my office with my heart in my throat and Peter on my mind and as I moved with the masses down what seemed like an endless nine flights of emergency stairs, I realized that each day is precious. I can still hear the click, click, click of my heels on the stairs and I can still recall thinking that if this was my last day on earth, I had not lived it the way I wanted. But Peter had. Even though his life had ended way too early, I knew that each day for him was exceptional. And I was spending each precious day bored and not contributing to the world in the best way I could.

As I exited the dark stairway into the bright sun, I made the decision to quit my job. I had been toying with the idea for a long time but in that moment I knew it was time to stop waiting for the perfect moment. Because we never know if that moment is going to come or how many moments we have left. I left my job a short time later with a few thousand dollars I had saved up and some baking skills I had learned from classes and a weekend job. I quickly pulled together a plan for a dessert catering business, something that I was far more passionate about than human resources.

I also began the journey of discovering myself. Because I knew that while I felt a tug towards baking, it was not really what I was all about. I knew there was more to me than that. But I didn't know what.

My first big ah-ha came when I picked up a little book called *The Alchemist* by Paulo Coelho. I want you to read the story for yourself, but I will tell you that it left me with the idea that deep down inside we each know the direction to our own greatest self. But often when we are faced with a decision, we fail to follow our own instincts and knowledge in favor of what is expected. But if you can discover your authentic self and let it guide your direction, your journey will be exceptional. I guess you could say that *The Alchemist* is what sparked this entire book you are now reading!

Armed with this idea that deep, down inside I knew the path I wanted to take, I began to put great focus on discovering my authentic self.

I started studying astrology, first in those daily Yahoo! horoscopes and then by making my own charts. It helped me immensely to realize my character and my talents. (Did you know that the configuration of the planets the moment you are born can shed so much light on what you have been gifted with? Give it a try sometime!)

I picked up a book on Buddhism called *The Beginners Guide to Walking the Eightfold Path* by Jean Smith. It really helped me to understand that so much of what was holding me back was in my own mind, that I was creating my own suffering. A daily meditation practice helped me to be able to listen to myself and work out issues and challenges in a way that feels good to me.

I connected with an old friend and a glimpse at her life woke me up to the fact that my life was lacking happiness. So I got back into dance and took up yoga and made time to read every night and started to travel again.

Having kids made me realize a whole new level to myself. My desire to help kids be their true selves. My desire to help them be safe being vulnerable. My desire to save them from my own mis-steps.

Throughout this whole journey, I shared what I learned with friends, with my kids, with readers of my blog, and with my Instagram followers. I love setting transformation in motion ! All of a sudden, I remembered how, from the time I was little, I wanted to be a teacher.

And most recently I happened upon an organization called Mindvalley and the amazing courses they offered, specifically Jon Butcher's *Lifebook*, helped me to open my eyes. I started to see how to put all the aspects of my life together into my own vision.

Through all of these experiences and countless more books and courses and quiet moments with myself, I discovered my authentic self... what I loved, what made me happy, how I wanted to impact the world, what I was good at, and what made me feel accomplished. And I put these parts of myself together to create a unique direction for my life.

I am so grateful that I discovered that we (each and every one of us!) can have the exceptional life I described, if we get to know ourselves. Your journey will look vastly different than mine but I promise it will be just as rewarding.

Some People Never Wake Up

Sadly, I have spent my life surrounded by far too many adults who, like I was, are living lives that are not their own. I have a friend who reads twenty fashion magazines every month cover to cover but works selling insurance and drags herself home every night. Then there is the guy down the street who spends every waking moment watching or playing sports but who works as a waiter and lives only for the weekend. And my cousin who wants to be outside all of the time but instead is a technology consultant trapped at her desk sixty hours a week . If you take a few minutes, I bet you can name a few people you know like this.

Insurance saleswoman, waiter, and technology consultant are not bad lives...for the right people. But these folks never took the time to get to know their authentic selves and discover their unique directions. They listened to what others thought was important and are now doing jobs and living lives that bring them only hints of joy. They are living lives full of complaints and regrets. And some of them, I fear, will never wake up to the realization that they can actually figure out what they are all about. I fear they will never wake up and live lives that support that.

Let me tell you a story about an exceptional group of young adults who started living lives that were not their own but happily did wake up.

When I was in middle school I was accepted to a very selective academic summer program offered by Johns Hopkins University. We lucky few got to spend three weeks living on a college campus and taking advanced classes in all sorts of disciplines. One year I took archeology, another time computer science, geometry for a session, and one year I studied logic and problem solving. It was an amazing experience for so many reasons but none more than the people I met.

I fell in with a group of people who are still my friends today. They were all super smart. But they were also creative. And determined. And funny. And philosophical. And curious. They were artists and poets and comedians and healers and travelers and fashionistas and writers and athletes and math geeks. We were all so clear on what we loved and pursued it and shared it with a passion.

And we loved to learn, whether in class or just while we were hanging out on the quad. Some of us wrote songs. Some of us planned weekend field trips for the group. One of us designed dresses for everyone for the last dance. Some of us devised elaborate cheating systems for our bridge game. One of us created an ultimate frisbee league. All while completing high school and college level courses in three weeks.

I knew that these people were going to do great things in the world.

We all stayed in touch through high school and saw each other off to schools like Cornell, Penn, Harvard, and Berkeley. We put aside our passions for art and philosophy and sports and the harp and instead majored in engineering and biology and pre-law. Because we were the best and the brightest, the most talented minds and that is what the best and brightest are supposed to do. We graduated and moved into jobs with investment banks, prestigious law firms, university research programs, and global consulting agencies. We were sharing our most praised talents with the world.

We all mostly lost touch after we started work but then came the miracle of Facebook and we all rapidly reconnected after almost twenty years.

And we were all so very changed. Almost all of us had left our jobs and forsaken our degrees because we had all hit a point of realizing that those degrees and jobs were never our dreams. They were the dreams of our parents and of society. They were what we "should" have done because of our coveted talents but not what we wanted to do in our hearts.

We were now travel writers and creators of alternative schools and midwives and chefs and meditation instructors. We are happier and making a far bigger difference in the world doing what lights us up than when we were doing jobs that had been the dreams of someone else.

Just imagine if we had not been encouraged to push aside our own authentic dreams from the very beginning?!

Nobody Wants You to Paddle Your Own Canoe

Have you ever read the quote, "Love many, trust few, and always paddle your own canoe?" It is an old proverb that means be kind, don't be naive, and take responsibility for yourself.

Let's be real here. Most people in your life don't really want you to take responsibility for yourself. They are afraid you are going to make a mistake or a bad choice. They want you to follow their plans for you. And then when you follow their directions, well... they will praise you for your "independence!"

Note: While I am trying to get my point across, I do wholeheartedly admit that there are parents, teachers, friends, and companies that do actually want you to paddle your own canoe. They have put your needs above their own and are rooting for you to be you. If you come in contact with these amazing beings, stay close to them and show your immense gratitude in whatever way you can.

Now back to those who want to take the paddles!

Since you were in diapers you have probably been listening to so many other people's ideas about what you should be doing that you have not been able to listen to your own. It may have started from your youngest years when your teachers directed you to activities, your parents directed you to friends, and society directed you to the clothes you wore. Your desire for painting might have been squashed because your teachers saw your talent for math. You might have wanted a playdate with Sam but your parents thought Jane was a more well-adjusted kid so that is who you played with. Your love affair with your beat-up and torn jeans was ended by the bullying-fashionista-down-the-street's disdain for grunge.

While they will probably never admit it, and they may not even realize it, almost everybody is motivated to keep you from taking responsibility for yourself. You are a reflection of your parents, so most parents want you to be someone that Grandma and the guy who delivers the mail thinks is neat, clean, well-mannered, smart, and successful. Your teachers are graded on your performance, so want to put you in the position to be the kid who creates projects and test scores that impress the administration. Society wants to sell you the next hot sneaker, so they want you to be the person who needs whatever your neighbor has. Everyone wants to take the paddles away from you because they have your direction all planned out.

But stop! Stop leaving yourself open to the directions of others! Don't simply be a passenger in the canoe. Take the paddles and steer your own life.

It will mean turning in directions that might go against the desires and expectations of your families and communities.

Would you rather be in acceptance of yourself or in agreement with what the people around you are expecting? You only get one life! So, don't give up control to others. Stop waiting for someone to give you permission to act on your dreams. Take responsibility and create a life that is unique to you, a life that is exceptional.

The power to live an exceptional life lies in your hands. Decide to steer your own canoe.

The sad reality is that so many people make the big mistake of not knowing who they are. Or even worse, knowing who they are and putting it aside because it is not who they "should" be. So much of young adulthood is spent rejecting who you are because it is different from what your parents, schools, and society want for you.

You have picked up this book because you don't want to make that mistake. You want to know who you are.

4.

"You Are Expected to Be Mediocre."

"There are thousands of paths that lead to happiness, don't just accept one."

– Unknown

A lot of people believe there is only one acceptable path in life. I say choose your own.

There Is Not Only One Road

The people in your life are motivated to have you follow the same direction that everyone else does. It saves them a lot of embarrassment and pain.

The direction they think you should take usually consists of going to the best college you can get into or afford and then taking the highest paying or most prestigious job offered to you. This direction is really popular because it limits the risk for embarrassment. For you, and by extension, the people who are responsible for you.

When you do the same thing that everyone else is doing, you don't stand out. For better or worse. You may not create a brilliant innovation, but you also probably won't be laughed at for a spectacular failure. You won't be an embarrassment.

There is also tremendous pressure in our current world to find a "secure" life. A life that is fairly predictable. A life that is neither too good nor too bad, just nice and mediocre. This direction is very popular among parents because it avoids the risk of pain and discomfort for you, their darling child, and by extension, themselves.

This secure life usually looks a lot like your parents' life, without any of the negatives. They want you to have the parts of their life that are not painful and to have you correct any of the more painful parts. If your parents have a nice house in a decent neighborhood with kids and a dog and a job with a pension, then that is what they picture for you. Except maybe with a slightly bigger house in a better neighborhood, so that you can have the prestige they were sad they didn't have and a slightly bigger 401K, so that you don't have to scrimp as much as they do in retirement. Dog and kids included.

It feels secure. And safety and security is, for many parents, their biggest dream for you. (We'll talk about this much more in the chapter Do Away with Resistance". But just know for now that many parents would really like you to follow a path that offers the least risk for you to be poor, homeless, and hungry. You won't be in pain and neither will they.)

However, when you follow the same path as everyone else you lose the ability to be exceptional. Miguel Ruiz, the author of *The Four Agreements*, said it best. "Too many of us, rather than create our own work of art, emerge into life like photocopies. We template our lives based on the lives lived by people around. We emulate our fathers and mothers, our media and television—our goals therefore, are not our own, but merely suggestions from the people and ideas we sometimes blindly emulate. And, so, billions of people live a life that is not their own. Rather than listen within to what their heart or soul is asking them to do, they enter the giant human photocopier machine and emerge with a templated life."

It takes loads of courage to stay off the beaten path. There can definitely be some "down" moments filled with embarrassment and discomfort.

But taking the well-traveled path can just be the path to mediocrity and sadness.

The Pitfall of the Well-Traveled Path

My friend Janet traded her dream for the path everyone else was taking. I met Janet on vacation when I was about thirteen years old.

Janet was tiny. Janet was bold. Janet could read an entire book in a day. Janet was confident. Janet loved Pop Tarts. Janet was creative. Janet was brilliant. Janet French-braided hair like a boss.

Janet and I talked about boys. And the latest teen heartthrob. And how to put on lip gloss.

But what really stood out about Janet was how much she loved theater.

Janet and I were friends all through middle and high school. We saw each other each summer. We visited each other at home during the year. We wrote letters every week and talked on the phone well into the night until one of us started snoring.

All through high school I got a front row seat to Janet's love of theater. She was always involved in a play at school or in her community. Sometimes she was on the stage and a lot of the time she was behind it or in the front of the house. But she was always involved. Sometimes with more than one show. And she was always excited. She completely lit up when she talked about her current production.

I could not wait to hear all of the details because it was always so exciting! I can still picture the pages and pages of handwritten letters talking about the play she was working on. Or the pictures she included of all the great people she was working with. Or her hands gesturing wildly when she was trying to describe a certain dramatic scene or hilarious backstage fiasco.

I should also note that no matter how much schoolwork she had to maintain her straight A's, she always found time for the theater.

When it came time to apply for college, Janet did exactly what I expected she would do. She applied to a top school to prepare to be a doctor. The same thing all her cousins and friends were doing. The exact plan her parents had dreamed up for her since she was a baby.

It was expected, because working in theater was not the secure job that she was expected to get. It was just a dream. A dream with a lot of potential for failure. And dreams had no place in a comfortable future. A life in theater was the quick way to a life of poverty and instability. That life would have been so painful to Janet's parents that they certainly did not wish that on their daughter. They wanted to know that after four years in a top college Janet would get in to a good medical school and after that would be accepted into a good practice and would have a beautiful home and family. They wanted to know that Janet would be safe and successful.

But the Universe gave Janet a second chance. She came down with a wicked case of pneumonia the summer before college and had to defer her admissions. And for a year she worked in theater full-time after she recovered. I visited her a few times and I have to admit, I was more than a little jealous. I was in school struggling to learn about engineering, but Janet was off living her dream. She was working at a theater in Philly, up until all hours of the night, trotting around the city for props and costumes, living with a bunch of actors. She just bubbled over with excitement about what she was doing and learning. She was full of such energy that she practically glowed when you looked at her. I can still picture her today, dramatically telling me about what she was going to be doing that weekend at the theater with her hair a wild mess and a fire in her eyes, her gestures huge, leaning towards me with a huge smile on her face.

A year later she was at a top-notch school studying to become a doctor. All of the light had left her. She was cold and gray and bored and a little angry. I can still picture her. Hair pulled back severely. Lips tight. Quiet. Preoccupied. We drifted apart.

I reconnected with Janet a few years ago. She is now a doctor at a very prestigious practice. She makes a lot of money. Important people are beating down her door to be their doctor. She has a big apartment in a fancy zip code. Her kids go to an excellent private school She is secure and the vision of success. By her parents' standards, the standards she adopted.

But Janet is not happy. When I see Janet, she is lifeless and pale. The last time we had dinner with friends she talked about how tired she was and how she never sees her kids and about dealing with insurance companies and about colleagues she doesn't like. She listened to my two friends and I talk about how we had left our unsatisfying jobs to do things that were in alignment with our authentic selves and she wished out loud that she could do the same.

I felt such sadness that she had such a great passion and she turned her back on that dream for the security and safety of the colorless life that she has now.

There is an expectation that we follow in Janet's footsteps of security and success. But you don't have to.

A Tale of Two Siblings

I want to tell you the story of someone who didn't follow expectations. My brother.

But first, me. I did what everyone else like me did. I used good grades and excellent SAT scores to go to an Ivy League school and study engineering like my parents dreamed. After graduation I got a job at a company that employed probably 50% of people from my major even though I didn't understand what I would be doing and the only thing that sounded appealing was the salary. I followed everyone else because I didn't know I had the choice not too. And I made my parents proud and I didn't die.

My brother somehow knew that you didn't have to follow everyone else! He also started college studying something that didn't excite him at a college that didn't fit him. But after maybe a year, he listened to his inner voice tell him college was not for him and followed it right off the campus and off the path that everyone else was on.

He became a waiter. For a long time. And let me tell you, my parents were stewing in fear of embarrassment and discomfort. As he became aware that he loved the food industry by hanging out with chefs and cooks late into the night, he began focusing on learning restaurant management and started working at nicer restaurants.

He moved in to assistant manager positions and finally became a general manager. He was following his own unique direction without regard to the path he was "supposed" to be on and when it told him it was time to move on, he would leave his job and find the next place he was meant to be. He moved between restaurants and was, more than once, unemployed as he looked for the next step in his journey. Again, not the path the majority of people in his life were taking. Most of us were finding that one job and sticking to it until retirement.

Recently, his inner voice told him to head to Charleston where there is a cool, up-and-coming food scene. He traveled down to Charleston and visited dozens of restaurants that he had heard about. He talked to the owners and managers and made some great friends and connections. He landed a job managing a restaurant that was not yet open but would grow to be one of the hottest new places in Charleston and happen to be crowned one of the best burgers in the U.S. in 2018! And then he left.

Again, following his own unique direction, not the more well-traveled path of staying put when you have a good thing going. And he opened his own pop-up restaurant making Jersey style sandwiches. Cheesesteaks, rubens, meatball parm. And it is on fire! This year I bet his will be one of the 50 best cheesesteaks in the country!

My brother definitely did not follow the path that most of his peers followed or the path our parents would have liked for him. He is proof that going in your own unique direction is absolutely a path to a life of joy. He owns his own restaurant, cooks the food he loves while still getting to be out front and talking to people who love food, and gets to work with his wife (who also happens to be his best friend).

My brother knew who he was, set a path for himself that let him grow and give, and he now lives a joyful exceptional life of his choosing.

So much of young adulthood is about figuring out how to fit yourself into the same mold as everyone else. Everyone strives to look a certain way, possess certain material goods, achieve certain awards and grades. And then when we reach adulthood we look out from behind the mask we created and feel empty. Because all that was truly "us" has been removed or hidden way. And we spend the next few decades reclaiming who we are and what we love. We strive for the uniqueness that we lost. We no longer want to be mediocre.

But you are the only one who can decide what makes you feel joyful. What feels painful to your parents may not feel painful to you. What is

embarrassing to your friends may not be
embarrassing to you.

Just because everyone else chooses to do or
believe something, does not make it right.
Remember when most people believed that the
earth was flat? Not last I checked! So let go of
the idea that you need to be on the same path as
everyone else and jump into this book to find
your own.

5.

"Mediocre is Okay."

"Life is either a daring adventure or nothing at all."

- Helen Keller (author, political activist, lecturer)

You might be thinking that this exceptional life thing seems like a lot of work on your part. And maybe it's easier to go along with what everyone else is doing. Take the path that is already laid out for you. Let somebody else make the decisions for you. But it is not! Why? Because mediocre is not okay! And even if you aren't embracing this concept right now, I promise you that one day you will. So do the work now and start enjoying your life today!

Mediocre Can't Change the World

Albin de la Simone, a French songwriter, once said, "Being my own self, I am useful." When we are each sharing our unique gifts, our authentic self, with the world, we are truly useful to humanity. And I believe that our basic desire is to share our true selves. To be driven and focused and committed. To be undeterred and unable to be distracted from sharing what lights us up inside. To change the world for the better.

And by changing the world, I do not mean you have to do something as grand as colonizing Mars. Although, feel free if that is your calling! You can change the world by finding the perfect shoes to sell to each customer. You can change the world by creating an app that makes kids love math. You can change the world raising compassionate kids. You can change the world with one piece of art. The size and scale of what you do is not important. Changing the entire world or changing one person's world does not matter. The purpose is to create change.

Have you ever noticed the difference between a waiter who is clearly concerned with doing a "good" job to get a good tip and the waiter who takes joy in creating an amazing experience for you? The guy who is focused on giving you an unforgettable experience with his courtesy and promptness and interest in you will most likely get the best tip you can give and maybe even a good word to the manager or a recommendation to others. That waiter who is sharing his authentic self with you is changing your life for the better. His sparkle lights you up. It is a bit of an energy exchange!

Steve Jobs said, "The only way to do great work is to love what you do. If you haven't found it yet, keep looking. Don't settle. As with all matters of the heart, you'll know when you find it. And, like any great relationship, it just gets better and better as the years roll on. So keep looking until you find it. Don't settle."

Mediocre is a Life of Suffering

Sadly, through fear, we lose that desire to share our unique gifts and all try to be the same, and in that way cease to really be useful to society. People who don't believe that being their authentic selves is important and those who won't take the risk to find their authentic selves are not going to change the world. You just can't if you heart and soul is not in what you are doing.

Do you know that 87% of people have admitted to being "emotionally disconnected from their workplaces and less likely to be productive?" It's true according to a 2013 Gallup poll. And it's an accepted fact that people who are happier, do their jobs better.

When we are living lives that are not honoring our authentic self and aligned with our unique direction, we suffer psychologically. Research suggests that authentic self-expression is a necessary part of well-being. So to live an exceptional life full of joy you have got to be doing what lights you up inside!

I recently heard a story about three masons building a cathedral. It perfectly illustrates how the same work can provide you with a terrible life, a mediocre life, or an exceptional life. It all depends on how aligned it is with your unique direction.

A man came across three masons who were working on building a cathedral. The men were chipping away at huge blocks of granite.

The first seemed unhappy at his job, chipping away, muttering under his breath, taking frequent breaks. When the man asked what it was that he was doing, the first mason responded, curtly, "I'm hammering this stupid rock, and I can't wait until I can go home."

A second mason, seemingly more interested in his work, was hammering diligently and when asked what it was that he was doing, answered, "Well, I'm molding this block of rock so that it can be used to build a wall. It's not bad work, but I'll sure be glad when it's done."

A third mason was hammering at his block fervently, taking time to stand back and admire his work. He chipped off small pieces until he was satisfied that it was the best he could do. When he was questioned about his work he stopped, gazed skyward and proudly proclaimed, "I...am building a cathedral!"

The first mason was doing the work just to be paid. He hated it. This was hard work for him. He was suffering.

The second mason wanted to do a good job. But his heart was not really in it. His work gave him no joy. He too was suffering, just perhaps a bit more silently.

But the third mason, embraced his work. He loved building. And he did not mind the physical difficulty or the presumed heat or the probable long hours. His passion was building and while he might have aspired to be the architect one day, the work he was doing now was aligned with what he loved and was moving him in his unique direction. Even though he was doing the same work as the other masons, he was not suffering in the least.

And then one day, the architect of the cathedral was touring the site. He saw the first mason and his poor attitude and fired him because he was bringing down the energy of the team. He barely saw the second mason as he just blended in with every other man chipping away at the stone. But at the third mason he stopped. He could see the passion that this mason had and the value he was adding to this simple task. That mason was promoted on the spot to a position that allowed him to continue learning and growing in the direction of his passion.

Don't suffer by living a life that is not yours. Find a direction that allows you to be joyful and exceptional every single day.

Mediocre is a Life of Regret

Memento Mori. Have you ever heard that expression? It means "remember death". It is the practice of reflecting on your mortality. We each only have so much time on this earth and none of us know exactly how much that will be. So don't save living an exceptional life for the end.

"Let us prepare our minds as if we'd come to the very end of life. Let us postpone nothing. Let us balance life's books each day. ... The one who puts the finishing touches on their life each day is never short of time," says the ancient Roman philosopher, Seneca.

Look, you aren't guaranteed a "later" so start now. I get that you are not going to achieve all of your bucket list items right away, but know what you want to experience in life, know your authentic self and start living it now. Live life on your own terms. Now!

Don't look back at the end of your life and wish you had done it differently. Bronnie Ware is Australian nurse who has taken care of patients in the last weeks of their lives and written the book The Top Five Regrets of the Dying. She discovered that the top regret that people have on their deathbed is "I wish I'd had the courage to live a life true to myself, not the life others expected of me."

So honor your true self and follow your own unique direction, from this moment on. No regrets!

Mediocre Sets a Poor Example

When we embrace a life that is different from what everyone else is doing, we make that path more acceptable and accessible to others.

Think back to your history class. Women voters. Civil rights. The LGBT movement. It took a few brave individuals to insist on following their own unique path to inspire a dozen other people to follow theirs. Then hundreds and thousands and millions. Without those courageous people our progress as humans would have been far slower or maybe we wouldn't have achieved those things at all.

Giving up your own self to follow the dreams of others and settle for mediocre, is not only awful for you but also lousy for all the others who look to you as an example, today and in the future.

Don't settle for mediocre.

6.

"Life is a struggle."

"To achieve your dreams, work is required.
Suffering is optional."

- Jack Canfield (motivational speaker)

So many people truly believe that life can't be easy.
I don't.

It Has to Hurt

Do you remember that story your grandfather told you when you complained about waiting outside for the school bus on a cold day? The one about how he had to walk to school six miles (and ten on the way back!) with only one shoe on in a blizzard, every day? The reason for that story was to remind you that anything worth having requires hard work.

Ummmm, nonsense.
Did Grandpa's frostbitten toes really make his day at school more successful than the kid who had fur lined boots and a ride to school? Nope. It might have even made his day less successful.

That is because there is this false belief that is lingering out there in the world that you have to suffer for success. That there is something wrong with you if you are a travel blogger and you are roaming around the world eating fabulous food and staying in sweet hotels and laying on the beach all day. That there is something wrong with holing up in a cozy cabin in the woods to write a book. That there is something wrong with working from home on an alternate work schedule that allows time for preschool pickup and yoga class. That there is something wrong with not suffering.

The belief is that it is far more noble to suffer at a job you hate all day to collect your Friday paycheck until retirement. That you will achieve far more success with a seventy hour work week. That you will amount to nothing unless you are exhausted at the end of the day.

I don't agree. Life doesn't have to be so hard.

There Is Hard Work and Then There is Working Hard

Let's get one thing straight. You can't be lazy. That gets you nowhere. You do actually have to work hard. You just don't need to engage in hard work.

Confused?

Whatever you choose to do you need to work hard to make an impact. You cannot just sit around waiting for the universe to deliver your every desire on a silver platter. You need to put in the effort.

That travel blogger? She has to sit down and write. And edit. And schedule her travel. And set up meetings with people. And be observant. And handle of the travel issues that are sure to arise. She isn't just sitting on the beach. She is working hard. And if she is going to be successful at living the lifestyle she wants, she is going to work very hard. But because she loves what she does, it does not feel like hard work.

Compare that to the woman who decided to be a teacher for the pension but really does not like kids. Boy, does every day feel like hard work to that gal.

You can relate. Picture the thing you love to do most in the world and the thing you love to do least. Picture yourself doing the one you love for an entire day. Picture yourself putting everything you have into it. Did you see yourself smiling and enthusiastic? And utterly exhausted at the end of the day? But so pumped that you still have the energy to go out that night? That, my friend, is working hard.

Now picture yourself spending the day doing what you like least. I bet your grump face is on full display. At the end of the day do you see yourself just drained and cranky? Unable to even motivate yourself to head out to your favorite after work activity? That, sadly, is hard work.

Choose to work hard. At something that feels like play!

Stop Fighting

Now, a little bad news. That "work hard" vs "hard work" thing does not just happen because you are doing something you like. It is actually all in your mind.

I have a friend Sandy. Sandy is a photographer. She loves photography and is very talented at it. She loves to take photos of dead birds. But she believes that struggle equals success so she is always attracting struggle.

Sandy passes on opportunities for cool assignments that would let her travel because she is afraid they won't pay enough. Every time she has a problem with her camera it is "the end of her business." Instead of being confident in her own work she is constantly comparing her photos to those of other artists. Every hunch for a good photo she disregards because she doesn't think it will turn out right. She has wishes for her business but never takes action to move them forward. And she surrounds herself with people who harass her for taking a day off when she isn't feeling creative. Sandy never seems busy but every day is hard work for Sandy.

My friend Maverick is also a photographer. He loves photography and is also very talented, like Sandy. He loves to take photos of body parts. Maverick believes that life should be exceptional. And he attracts just that.

When a juicy assignment comes his way, he is on the next plane and sometimes sleeping that night under the stars and sometimes in a five-star hotel. Every problem with a camera is an opportunity to try a different one, sometimes even his phone. He could not care less about the work of other artists. He pulls out his camera almost every other minute and throws away hundreds of shots but often finds the perfect one when he wasn't looking. He has sensational friends who support his passion. Maverick is always on the move or in the darkroom or with a model. He works really hard and lives his dream.

There is nothing different about what Sandy and Maverick wanted to do for a job. They both wanted to take pictures. And there is practically no difference in how talented they are or how successful they are. The only difference was in their minds. Sandy expects life to be hard work. Sandy spent a lot of time in her own mind weighing the pros and cons of every option and looking at the worst-case scenario. Sandy's mind was engaged in really hard work. Maverick expects life to be exceptional. Maverick said yes to the things that came his way and operated from his heart instead of his mind.

Maverick was not fighting the gifts that were being given to him, he was taking them and working hard at them.

Over the past ten years I have developed lots of practices for working hard and working from my heart. I have learned how to make decisions easily, how to deal with challenges gracefully, how to not be sidelined by competition, how to be observant and grateful, how to listen to myself, how to get what I want, and how to support myself with relationships. Later in the book I will share them with you so that you can develop your own set of practices that will help you to live life with less struggle.

7.

There is a Better Way

"What if I fail? But oh my darling, what if you fly?"

– Eric Hanson (poet)

Steve Jobs said it so well. "Your time is limited, so don't waste it living someone else's life. Don't be trapped by dogma—which is living with the results of other people's thinking. Don't let the noise of other's opinions drown out your inner voice. And most important, have the courage to follow your heart and intuition. They somehow already know what you truly want to become. Everything else is secondary."

I have been on a breathtaking journey. One I needed to travel to be where and who I am today. I truly believe that my journey has shown me that my purpose in life is to help the youth of the world start farther ahead. Instead of spending decades finding your true self and then growing and having great joy, you will be able start from your true self and be able to experience deeper levels of growth and joy right now!

I am far from perfect but I have learned and figured out tons about living an exceptional life and I want to guide others so they have an easier path. I am continually creating a better version of myself by addressing issues that hold me back from being my authentic self and by learning new techniques to relate to the people and the world around me. I am always uncovering and refining and I hope you will do the same.

You can have an exceptional life by getting crystal clear on your authentic self. And once you have clarity on what lights your soul on fire, what your superpower is, how you want to serve the world, what success feels like to you, and what is essential to your happiness you will be able to set out in your unique direction in life. And when you follow that direction with courage and self-love you can live an exceptional life.

I want that for you.

PART III

DISCOVER YOUR AUTHENTIC SELF

Right now, I expect that you're very excited to start figuring out how you are going to live this exceptional life.

We are going to discover what you truly love, what you want to spend your time doing. We are going to pinpoint what you are great at and how you can bring that to what you love. Then we will look at how that all fits with how you want to change the world. And we will ensure that you are following your own values and making yourself happy while you do it.

Sound good?

8.

Passion

"You have to know what sparks the light in you so that you, in your own way, can illuminate the world."

- Oprah Winfrey (icon)

Discovering what you are passionate about is, to me, the most important part of knowing your authentic self.

Passion Lights Your Soul on Fire

Most people think that passion is the same as love. But it's more. It is a drive—to learn, to share, and to work hard at creating something.

Passion is Curiosity

Being passionate is being insanely curious. It means you want to learn everything you can about what you love.

So curious about something that you can read hundreds of books on it.

You love talking to people about it because you want to hear what they know.

You are always searching for YouTube videos and blog posts and podcasts on the topic.

You want to play around with making things related to your passion...just to see what happens.

You want to take a class a subject just for fun.

You learn about other people who are curious about your topic.

You travel far and wide to experience it in a new way.

When you are curious like my friend, Claire, who is so passionate about baking that she always smells like cake, watches tons of baking shows, always has her nose in a cookbook, is always making friends with the owners of every bakery she enters, and volunteers for organizations that help aspiring bakers. She is of course always baking. She is always taking a road trip near and far to try a bakery she has heard about. In the past month alone, she has had me try a brown butter donut from a carwash (surprisingly good!), an apricot pistachio tart from a little French hole-in-the-wall (as good as you would have expected!), and too many things to count covered in chocolate. I love watching her curiosity (and tasting it)!

When you are curious like my daughter with anime. Because she is homeschooled, she has a great deal of freedom to spend her time however she wants—which is quite often learning about anime. She watches anime cartoons and is constantly sketching in an anime style. Every drawing book she has is about anime, and she follows numerous anime artists on Instagram. She even stayed up an entire night to watch the new season of Voltron (an anime show) when it came out on Netflix at three in the morning!

And when you are curious like my brother who is so passionate about a good sandwich that he opened a pop-up restaurant that serves what could be the world's best cheesesteak. Wherever he goes he has to try a sandwich (maybe three) and photograph it. He makes friends with everyone who has ever made him a good sandwich, follows all sorts of food bloggers, and watches shows about food. When he finds his way into the cookbook section of a bookstore, watch out.

Curiosity is incredibly important because it allows you to continue learning. It keeps your mind active and observant and open to new possibilities. Walt Disney once said, "We keep moving forward, opening new doors, and doing new things, because we're curious and curiosity keeps leading us down new path."

Be curious. Never stop learning.

Passion Causes Excitement

Being passionate about something is being extraordinarily excited. It means you want to share what you love with the world. And that is good.

The other day I met someone who was so excited it rubbed off on me. His name is Jay Shetty and I was listening to his podcast while I went for a walk around town. And after sixty seconds I had to turn it off—because Jay was incredibly excited. And that made me excited. And I was eager to hear what he had to say, and I knew it was going to be transformative and give me insight. But I wanted to listen to it when I could give it my full attention.

So instead of listening to the podcast on my walk, I thought a bit about excitement.

About how, without even knowing the details of what he was going to say, I knew that I wanted to hear it.

Why was that? Because excitement means "I love this." And that tells me:

- That I might love it too,

- That you are so into it that you have really done your research so your recommendation is worth listening to,
- That your motivation is joy not manipulation.

This idea made me think back to when I moved into my house one November and there was no heat. It was a massive, rambling Victorian house and it was darn cold. I needed a plumber—ASAP. I didn't know anyone in the area so could not get a recommendation and I called every plumber in the book. At least five came by to look at my "chilly situation."

I hired Gary without even getting a price—because Gary was excited. He loved the old pipes in the Victorian house. He might have actually whispered to the broken furnace. He took the time to look at things from a variety of angles. He asked questions. He smiled. With enthusiasm, he told me his plan, the options and the pitfalls. Gary clearly loved plumbing. He made me love it. He made me confident that he was a plumbing expert. He made me feel like he wanted to do the job. So, I hired Gary.

I didn't hire the five other guys because they were mediocre. Plumbing was simply a job, not a passion. They were there to make money. They were not excited, and neither was I.

By the way, Gary not only did that plumbing job but pretty much re-piped our entire house. His work was impeccable. He settled for nothing less because it was his art, his passion. He came in the middle of the night—more than once. I recommended him to all my friends and neighbors. And when Gary passed on, I ended up with a mediocre plumber during a kitchen renovation (my contractor's choice, not mine) and his lack of excitement shows in the use of cheap pipes, the fact that my dishwasher leaks all over the floor on occasion, and the mess of pipe junctions all over my basement that make it terribly difficult to turn off the water in an emergency.

The moral of my story? Be excited. Be so in love with this thing that you want to tell everyone you meet about it.

Passion Fuels Persistence

Being passionate means you are willing to work hard, and you have the persistence to move forward in the area that you love.

It is difficult to work hard at something you don't really love. When you truly love something, you are happy to put your blood, sweat, and tears into it. You want to grow and achieve and you are enjoying what you are doing.

Remember when you were little and say, loved knitting? (Okay, so maybe we are talking about me when I was little.) Nobody had to tell you to, "go do your knitting." In fact, they probably had to tell you to stop! Nobody had to encourage you to learn a new stitch. You were probably begging Grandma to "show you how." Nobody had to tell you to correct your mistakes. You saw them for yourself and fixed them, so your scarf would be exceptional. You worked hard because you loved what you were doing.

When working toward achieving your goals, there is nothing more important than persistence. According to the book Grit: The Power of Passion and Perseverance, success is mostly about something called "grit" or the perseverance it takes to stick to your goals. And a person who is passionate also has perseverance.

My youngest daughter has "grit." She wants to be an actress and over the past year she has been doing some background work for TV and films. She loves it.

She's intrigued by the technical aspects and the craft services table (that the snack table for us non-actors) and the wardrobe people. She's always full of questions on the way home about what certain lingo meant or the resumés of the actors she got to work with that day. She likes that she gets paid. She doesn't mind wearing a winter coat on the subway in August or hiking back up the bunny slope thirty times in one day. She doesn't mind that sometimes there is hours of waiting around or that sometimes the scene she was in gets cut in the final edit. She loves every moment of it.

While I knew that she was curious and excited, it was only recently that I learned she had perseverance.

She got selected to work on a new Keanu Reeves movie overnight at Grand Central Station. We arrived at eight at night , met with the production assistant, makeup, and wardrobe and then waited. We walked over to the set to get a snack and waited. Then we went back to holding and waited. Then we got a lunch break at well past midnight and nibbled on some food while we waited. Then we went back to set and waited. And at 3am they told us they had to dismiss the kids because they could only work so many hours. So, back to holding we went to collect our things and sign out.

All around us the other kids were upset. One girl was mumbling under her breath that she can't believe she came all the way to New York City and wasn't even on camera. Two boys were actually borderline throwing a tantrum. Another boy was complaining about what a waste of time it was.

And my daughter stood in line to check out and said. "That was awesome. Wasn't the hotel ballroom a really nice holding room? How awesome was it that they had Pop-Tarts at the craft table? I wonder how that stunt they were filming is going to look in the movie? Wasn't the production assistant really nice? Did you have any of the blue cheese dressing at lunch because it was really good? Wasn't the guy on set playing the homeless man just perfect? How cool was it to be in Grand Central so late at night watching a movie being made?" And on, and on, and on.

As we waited in the parking garage at three in the morning (for our car to be jump started), I asked if her she was disappointed that she didn't get to be on camera and she looked at me and said, "Why would I be?" And that is the moment I knew that she has a passion for the business of film and TV. Because she had "grit," the perseverance, to keep going no matter how challenging the circumstances.

Be persistent. Be inspired to work for what you want.

Passion Doesn't Change

Your passion never changes. It evolves.

Our passions are in full swing by the time we are seven or eight years old—the time when we are most curious and excited and persistent. It is a time when we are allowed to "waste time" on almost anything we want so we pick what we love the most. It is a time before grades are important and activities are organized. It is the time before other people become involved in guiding us toward what they think is in our best interest. It is the time of your life when you can whole-heartedly say "I love soccer." Or reading. Or bugs. Or building things. Or watermelon.

Jake took his obsessive passion for Legos and let it evolve into a career in architecture. Ron started tracing animals his dad drew on the chalkboard when he was young and cultivated that into a career as a successful comic artist. And Bessie, a successful lawyer today, recalls that she didn't really have a passion, she was too busy always trying to do the right thing. Umm, Bessie? I think your passion has stayed the same!

A lucky few never lose their connection to their passion. But so many of us put it aside for something someone else has told us is more important. And after many years we forget our passion. But it is not gone. Your passion has not changed. It is still there—buried under years of being dismissed and rejected.

And if you tell me that your passion changed, I will tell you that it wasn't your passion to begin with. You are not yet remembering your true passion.

When I was seven years old, I wanted to be a teacher. My teachers were superheroes to me. I played teacher with my stuffed animals and my friends. I made pretend lesson plans and worksheets. (don't judge!) My favorite day of the year was helping my mom decorate and set up her classroom in August. But I let that passion for teaching go for a path that I thought would make better use of my talents and bring more money and glamor.

But guess what? Today I am a teacher. Not in the traditional sense. I homeschool my kids. I write a blog to teach other homeschool parents how to come up with exciting curriculum for their kids and another blog to teach people how to begin transforming their lives. I teach dance to kids at the local elementary school. And I hope I am teaching you with this book! My passion isn't exactly the same as it was when I was a little girl, it has evolved into the perfect fit for me.

When I look at what my two daughters were passionate about when they were eight years old it was dance for one and art for the other. And while they are only now in middle and high school, their passions have not changed. They have evolved. The dancer narrowed her passion down to musical theater and then opened it up to include acting and singing and now we might really call her passion, "performing." The artist clarified that her passion is not for all art but for "drawing." And as a parent, I balance carefully between supporting their passion with opportunities for growth while allowing them to explore other things that interest them so that they can continue to allow their passion to evolve.

Embrace the evolution of your passion—never believe it has disappeared.

Time to find out what you want to learn about, share, and work hard at.

Explore Your Passion

Time for the fun stuff! Discovering your passion.

We are going to try a few different exercises to uncover what may have gone into hiding.

As you complete these exercises, please do not pass judgement on what you are writing down. Do not dismiss anything as "unreasonable!" At this stage we are letting it all out and then we will come back and see what it all means and what direction it's pointing toward. It is important to allow your thoughts and feelings to come out and capture them in your journal.

If you are not honest, you are not going to be able to uncover your authentic self!

Your Passion Has Always Been with You

We just talked about how your passion never changes. So, it stands to reason that if you can remember what you were passionate about as a child, you will be able to more easily rediscover your passion.

In *Living Out Loud*, a fantastic book that helps you reclaim your playfulness, Keri Smith reminds us, "Children possess this divine awareness. They are naturally joyous and passionate. The also instinctively know what they want, and they find ways to act on their instincts, doing exactly what they want. Childhood memories carry us back to a time of inspiration, excitement, and joy. (They) ...allow us to remember a time when passion was foremost and to reconnect with our true selves—the part of ourselves that is not defined by family or financial or social obligations."

Let's go back to the time when what you wanted was more important than what grades you got or what rank you were or what your paycheck looked like. Let's remember what you are passionate about.

VISUALIZATION: "Childhood Dream"

Find a nice, quiet place and settle in with your journal. I am going to ask you to visualize your childhood self.

Begin to picture your third-grade, eight-year-old self.

Begin visualizing a normal school day. Picture yourself waking up and getting a reading assignment for school. Going to school. Your friends, recess, teachers, classes. Your after-school time... homework, playtime, chores. Close your eyes and watch yourself. Take notes as you go along, if you like.

Then visualize a typical weekend day. Picture what you liked to do when you weren't at school. Where did you go? Who did you spend time with? Take more notes.

When you are done, think back to what stood out as the most energizing and exciting part of your day. There will probably be many things that you liked, but what is the one magical thing that lit you up inside? Write about this in your journal.

Then visualize your eight-year-old self again. Picture yourself getting to spend an entire day doing that one magical thing. Take the time to sit with this vision until you can feel it all throughout your body. It is probably making you tingle with excitement! If not, try the exercise over again another day.

Write down this magical something in big letters on the page. Circle it, and label it "Passion."

The "Childhood Dream" exercise reminds you about what you were most passionate about before any constraints were put on you to "spend your time wisely." That passion still lives inside you today!

You Get Lost in Your Passion

When you are passionate about something you lose all sense of time. You find that you are so absorbed that you don't have interest in things that don't matter like social media, gossip, or self-comparison.

You find that you forget to eat. You find that you can stay up past your bedtime without a yawn.

Let's find out where you like to get lost.

FIELD TRIP: "The Bookstore Browse"

Schedule about an hour for this exercise. Grab your journal and head to the local bookstore. You are going to do a little browsing.

Once you get to the bookstore, I want you to wander through every single non-fiction section.

When you find a section that interests you, make note of the section and the time. Start browsing through some of the books. As you find specific books that interest you, make notes about them in your journal. When your interest has been satisfied in that section, make note of the time and move on to the next aisle.

After you have wandered through all of the non-fiction sections, grab a seat and look back at your notes.

What section did you spend most of your time in? Pick a blank page in your journal and write it down. If you had a couple that were pretty close, write them all down. If you found that you were focused on a sub-set of books in that section, write that sub-section down. You can have a few sections. Then circle that section (or sections) and label it, "Passion" so you can use it later.

"The Bookstore Browse" exercise is a great way to find what it is that you love to get lost in. If you can get lost in books about this subject, this is where you will happily get lost in life.

You Get Excited When You See Your Passion

Earlier in the chapter I told you that passion is excitement. It is something that makes you want to yell, "I love this!" You don't just get excited when you are doing it, you also get excited (and maybe a little jealous) when you see other people doing it.

Let's explore some of those people and what they are doing. It will give you a clearer vision of what you want to be doing.

EXERCISE: "I Envy Your Job"

Grab your journal and find a quiet place. Pick a blank page and divide it into two columns. You are going to take some notes on the people you envy.

Go through the list of people you follow on Instagram. If you envy their job, write their name in the first column. Try to come up with a list of at least twenty-five people (if you are not on Instagram, try to picture everyone you know… friends, family, celebrities).

Next, put your phone away and go back to your list. For each person, write down what their job or career is.

On a blank page, start clustering the jobs together based on similarity. Like "TV actor", "Broadway star", and "dancer" might go together for you into "performer." If you have a job that repeats for more than one person, add it to your cluster more than once. If you have some clusters that are somewhat similar, you might consider merging them together. Circle your biggest cluster (or clusters) and label, "passion."

"I Envy Your Job" can open your eyes to where you would want to spend your time.

Clear Away Your Fear So You Can See Your Passion

A lot of people can't see their passion because they are so focused on how to make money. I assure you that if you are working in an area that you are passionate about, success will come to you (and later in the book you may actually find out that, for you, money doesn't equal success).

Let's remove the fear of money and see what it uncovers.

EXERCISE: "All the Money in the World"

Grab your journal, pick a blank page, and start numbering each line 1 through 20. This is a "stream of conscious" exercise. No thinking—just write!

Take out your journal and write twenty things you would spend your forty hours a week doing if money were no object. No judgements—just write!

Now let's organize these activities. First, read through your list and cross off anything that you look at and think, "No, I would not really want to spend my day doing that." Cluster the remaining activities together into groups in any way that makes sense to you. Which group do you gravitate toward? Which group is the one you would want to spend your day doing? Circle the group that really speaks to you and label it, "Passion."

Taking away the pressure of money with the "All the Money in the World Exercise" lets you get in touch with what you would love to do with your life.

You discovered a lot about your passion and you already know yourself on a deeper level.

Now, let's make some sense of what you learned.

Your Unique Passion Discovered

You probably don't even need me to tell you this, but your passion has been revealed. It popped out in every exercise. It might need some fine tuning, but you now have a clear idea of what you really love.

Label a blank page in your journal "Passion" and bookmark it so you can find it later. Put a square in the center of the page. Now transfer everything you labeled as "Passion" from the previous exercises outside the square so that you can see everything all together. You may see a lot of the same "passions" or similarities between them.

Spend some time with this picture. Then let the words around the square guide you to write your passion or passions in the square.

You will probably have something a little vague at this point. But relax, this is not the end point, this is only the beginning.

At this point you might be thinking, "I can't have a job in 'reading' or 'dogs' or 'food.'" STOP! This is not the time to think about reality. This is the time to discover your passion. You may have reservations about pursuing a life in line with your passion, but you should have no reservations that this is in fact your passion. You have just shown yourself that you could spend tons of time learning about this, you envy people who get to do this, and this is how you would spend your days if you didn't have to earn a paycheck. This is in fact your passion.

Do not apologize for your passion or try to wish it away! The world needs people who are passionate about all sorts of things. Even when they are unglamorous. Like bugs or trash or other people's feet.

A word of warning though, if your passion is controlling you it is an addiction, not a passion. A passion is something you put time and energy into because you want to. You have a desire to learn about it, and share it with others, and work hard on it. An addiction is something you are putting your time and energy into because you "have to." You feel compelled to do it even if you don't want to and you put it above doing other things or spending time with others. An addiction can make your world smaller, not bigger.

There is a big difference in being passionate about video games and addicted to them. Being passionate about beer and being addicted to it. Being passionate about reading or addicted to it.

Do a double-check on your passion. And if you realize that your passion is really an addiction, talk to an adult about your concerns. A parent, a teacher, a family friend. They can help you to work towards letting go of your addiction.

That "follow your passion" mantra is a step in the right direction, but it is not the way to an exceptional life. It is only the beginning.

You are now in possession of the knowledge of what your passion is. What you want to learn about and share and work hard at.

But passion is only the beginning of discovering your authentic self. You need to know how to do what you are passionate about in your own unique way.

9.

Talent

"Everyone is gifted. But some people never open
their package."

- Wolfgang Riebe (magician)

Your talents make up a big part of who you are.
They are the skills and abilities that we use to create exceptional
things in the world of our passion.

Your Talent is Your Superpower

I like to think of your talents like your superpowers. They are the
abilities you have that someone would call on you to use to help
make the world a better place. And just like real superheroes, we all
have our own unique superpowers.

Talents Are Building Blocks

You are not "talented" at your passion, you use your talents to let you live your passion. These many different talents make us each unique and differently abled.

Let's take dance as an example. Nobody is talented at dance. A bit contrary to what you have always been told, right? Let me explain.

Dance is a passion. They are talented at flexibility or balance or strength or musicality. They are talented at creative vision or organization or memorization. They are confident or dramatic or intuitive. Different combinations of these talents make for different dancers. A strong, confident, sassy, acrobatic dancer might fulfill her passion working on the hottest new Ariana Grande video. A flexible, intuitive, dramatic dancer might be touring with a contemporary dance company. And a musical, visionary, dramatic dancer might find happiness as a choreographer. All are living their passion for dance but in ways that are aligned with their unique talents.

And yes, there may be a set of common set of talents that most dancers possess, but that does not mean that you cannot dance unless you possess them all, it only means you are creating your own unique version of your passion using your unique talents. And the world needs more of that. That is how new ideas, inventions, and pieces of art are born.

And yes, I suppose you can say that you are talented at "dance" if you are talented at a lot of the qualities that go into dance. But try to keep in mind this new mindset you have learned about passion and talent.

Talents Come in All Shapes and Sizes

The world needs people of all different talents. You may have one talent or many talents.

You can have talents motivating others. Your talent could be charm, confidence, courage, or patience.

You can have talents that generate ideas. Your talent could be adventure, research, curiosity, or visioning.

You can have talents communicating. Your talent could be empathy, entertainment, public speaking, or personality.

You can have physical talents. Your talent could be speed, precision, flexibility, or hand-eye coordination.

You can have talents tackling projects. Your talent could be analytics, determination, discipline, or planning.

And the list goes on.

Do you want to know what my strongest talent is? Organizing. Yes, that is my talent.

One of my earliest memories was the first time I moved. I was probably three or so and I could not write yet. But I was determined to pack my room. I had a box and I was going to pack up all of my View-Master disks (A View-Master was like a portable slide show. It was a pair of goggles that you inserted a disk of tiny slides into and then you clicked through the slides and it was like you were in the Serengeti leaping alongside Spiderman. Think of it as an early version of VR goggles). I had a lot of View-Master disks and I wanted them organized for the move. I spent the afternoon labeling them all with my own faux version of cursive writing.

For my eighth birthday I asked for a filing cabinet, so I could keep all of my schoolwork organized.

Whatever career I found myself in—from computers to cakes, I used my talent for organization to streamline whatever process I was involved in to save myself and others lots of time and money.

Today I can be found organizing homeschool curriculums, family trips, this book, the silverware drawer, and even other people's closets. I can size up any problem and organize it into something that makes life easier.

Organizing is my superpower!

Your unique talents are what make you... YOU! They are what make you valuable to humanity. They are YOUR superpowers—different from those of Wonder Woman or Spiderman but just as important.

Embrace Your Unique Talents

Sadly, society does just about everything it can to turn each superhero into a robot. We look at certain talents and decide they are the ones that everyone should have.

It is like math.

Yes, every person on this planet benefits from learning basic math. We all add, subtract, multiply, and divide in our daily lives. We use money. We tell time. We use fractions and some basic geometry. We read charts and solve some basic algebraic equations. These are talents that serve us well.

And some people on this planet benefit from a lot more math. People who are interested in pursuing things like math and engineering and rocket science. These people need calculus and trigonometry and advanced calculus and super advanced calculus.

But we are ALL expected to leave high school with a fairly high knowledge of math—with far more trigonometry and calculus than most of us actually need in real life. And with the expectation of high grades in those subjects as well—regardless of what we want to pursue after high school.

Every time I work in the library there are at least a half dozen kids being tutored in math. Math homework brought weekly meltdowns in my own home while growing up. And why? So that everyone can be talented in math? It is incredibly sad to see kids sacrificing time building their own talents so they can spend their time trying to become talented at something they have no interest in or need for.

Albert Einstein wisely said, "Everyone is a genius. But if you judge a fish on its ability to climb a tree, it will live its whole life believing it's stupid."

Don't try so hard to fit into the box society tries to put you in. You'll miss out on contributing your greatest gifts to humanity. You'll be taking that path to mediocrity we talked about. So, stop trying to change yourself to be like everyone else and embrace what is uniquely you.

Talent Comes Easy. Or Maybe It Just Looks that Way.

What about a talent that you don't have? Out of luck? Because people are born with talent, right? Well, that's only partially true.

Every time we try something new it either comes easy for us or it is hard for us.

As children when we try something like reading or kicking a ball or shaking our bottom while dancing in the kitchen and we do it well because of a slight natural personality or physical trait, do you remember what happens? People go wild! "Oh my gosh! Look how he kicked that ball. He is going to become a great soccer player!" And who doesn't love praise? Even as a tiny person. We think we are amazing (...at everything). So, we usually do it again and again. And that, my friend, is our first experience with practicing.

In Malcolm Gladwell's book, *Outliers*, (a must read!) he explains that you need ten thousand hours of practice to become an expert. Which is really not a lot when you think about doing a certain activity from the time you were very small.

So, for some people that seem super talented at something, they may have had the advantage of a really good head start.

And the other kids? The unfortunate ones who tried something and didn't knock it out of the park on the first try? They were either ignored or told "keep trying" or even worse—no words of praise, no inspiration or motivation to keep trying or to start practicing.

But if there is a talent you want and don't have, you need to practice. And there is only one way to get in ten thousand hours of practice—motivation.

I learned this lesson about practice once I started homeschooling my kids. I want them to learn to become good writers because clear written communication is a talent worth having no matter what your passion. So, I often ask them to write reports. I found that I would ask them to write a report about a certain topic and it would be met with complaints and tears and crappy reports. But if I asked them to write about a topic that they were interested in, I would have to drag them away from their laptops. I received reports that I found interesting and informative. The report that they were interested in certainly provided them with a greater learning experience and much more practice.

Practice what you want to be talented at. Do it wherever and whenever you can. Watch videos. Read books. Hang out with people who can do it. Take classes. If you truly love it, all of this will feel like play and not like work! And through all that play, you will become much more capable.

Even superheroes (like you) need to work out!

You Stink at What You Love

When you pursue your passion but forget about using your talent, you are not setting yourself up for an exceptional life.

Sometimes you are fortunate and are really good at what you love. It feels like it comes easy to you. But other times you love something and don't feel like you have enough talent to pursue that passion. What should you do?

What you are passionate about is what you should do—no exceptions.

Passion is the place where you want to spend your time. But how you spend your time within your passion, depends on your talents. And if feel like you stink, you are just not using your talents.

I have a friend, Deirdre, who was a talented artist. Art was undoubtedly her passion. She studied art in school and it seemed as if she painted all day every day. She visited every museum she could. She painted breathtaking landscapes that collectors bought and hung in galleries. And she wanted to share her passion for art.

So, she opened an art school... and it bombed. She was disappointed by how unmotivated the kids were. She could never pay the rent because she didn't invoice her students on time. She let students take advanced classes even if they couldn't draw a stick figure and then lost her more advanced students because they weren't challenged. She didn't understand what was wrong. Art was her passion! How could her art school be failing?

Deirdre was not using her talents. She was a talented painter and was gifted in making connections in the art world. She was not a talented teacher, accountant, or disciplinarian. She was not organized or able to use technology or be on time. She was trying to enjoy her passion in a way that asked her to use skills that she didn't have. And she closed her business—thinking she stunk at art.

But Deirdre's story could have had a different ending. If she had acted as director of the art school and taught art history to the students and took them on field trips to museums and brought in the art critics she knew to help her students, she would have been using her talents. If she had brought in a talented art teacher and an organized office administrator, she would have been filling the other roles in her business with people who had the skills that she lacked.

Deirdre made a fatal error. She knew she had a passion for art, but she made the mistake of thinking that meant that the talents required to be a painter were the same talents required to be an art teacher.

Not everyone is talented at everything. To live your passion in an exceptional way you have to find out how to use your unique talents properly.

It's time to find out what your superpowers are!

Explore Your Talent

Throughout my life, I have always loved an exercise that helps me to discover my talents—showing me new areas that I might want to grow and explore.

As you go through the exercises, capture your talents in your journal. Don't dismiss anything as silly. You are gathering information at this point. We will fine tune it all later.

Help!

Your friends might have more clarity on your talents than you do! They absolutely know your superpower and what kind of crisis they would call you to help with. Do they call you when they have a frozen computer screen? Or when they need a ride? Or a shoulder to cry on? Or a book recommendation? To quiz them for a test? They know what you are great at.

So, let's ask them by using an exercise based on that hilarious old game show, *Match Game*. (Check it out on YouTube when you have a minute!)

ASK A FRIEND: "Match Game"

This exercise is best done over social media, but you can do this exercise in person if you prefer.

Post the following statement. "Please answer the following question. If I needed help with _____, I would ask <insert your name> because <he or she> is _____."

You can add a little clarification on why you are doing this if that makes it

---

easier! And you can always provide an example like, "If I needed help with babysitting, I would ask Kim because she is great with kids."

Once you have gotten at least fifteen responses, write them down in your journal. Group them into, "Like," talents such as communication skills, creativity, etc. There is not a right or wrong to the group these together. It can be general or specific—whatever feels right to you. Then circle the three groups that had the greatest number of items and label them, "Talent."

The "Match Game" exercise is a great way to see talents that you have that you might never have thought of as talents.

So Proud

Just like your passion, many of your talents began to appear and take shape when you were very young. This exercise will help you to remember what some of those talents were.

Let's head back in time and remind you of what makes you stand out.

EXERCISE: "Good Grades"

You are going to make a list in your journal of all of your top grades, awards, praise, and achievements. Start from the present and work backward year by year, as far back as you can remember.

Think about the classes where you received the highest grades and note what skills you used to get those grades: memorization, creative projects, descriptive writing, eloquent speeches. What did your teacher praise you for?

Think about any awards you won for academics or sports or arts or community service and again what skills were being awarded: speed, emotion, drawing, compassion.

Think about praise your parents gave you and what was it for: helping with your siblings, being on time, improving your grades.

And think about any other achievements you had that year and what skills were being utilized.

When you are done, use a new page to write down your skills and group those together that have similar traits. Again, the groups you create should make sense to you. Circle the three groups that have the greatest number of items and label them, "Talent".

"Good Grades" can trigger your memory to where your talents lie.

Singing Your Praises

This exercise makes people a little uncomfortable because you have to listen to wonderful things about yourself. However, it is one of the best ways I have found to uncover your greatest talents.

Pick three friends and let's get started!

After this exercise you will not only know more about your talent, but you will feel pretty darn good about yourself!

ASK A FRIEND: "Honesty Hour"

Schedule one-on-one time with three or more of your friends. You can do this in person or over the phone. You are going to ask your friend to talk for three minutes about what you do really well.

Grab your journal and be ready to write. Let your friend know that they have to talk about all the things you do really well (and you are not allowed to respond). Set your timer for three minutes and then be silent! Listen and record what your friend tells you. When the timer goes off, they have to stop.

When you have had all of your sessions, use a blank journal page to write down all of the talents that came out, grouped by similarity again. Then circle the 3 groups that have the most items and label them "Talent."

"Honesty Hour" is a great way to get into a stream of consciousness about your talent!

Test Your Way to Talent

Sometimes a test is a useful way to uncover your talents. Here are a couple of online resources to help you explore.

Genius U helps you determine which of four types of genius is your natural genius and then tells you more about what talents that genius type possesses. You can take a short, one-minute evaluation at www.geniusu.com and then I suggest taking the free course, *Live Like a Genius.*

StrengthsFinder is a great assessment to find out what makes you unique and powerful. You can find out your top five strengths for $19.99 at www.gallupstrengthscenter.com or get a more thorough evaluation for $49.99.

After either of these exercises, record the talents that you found and group similar items together. Circle the 3 groups that had the most items and label them, "Talent."

Taking a talent assessment is an easy way to open your eyes to what you are good at.

You have now discovered what your greatest talents are.

Let's clarify that information into something you can use to set a direction for your life.

Your Unique Talent Discovered

I hope that you had a lot of fun getting in touch with so many of your talents and seeing why you are such a superhero! Now let's put them together into something you can actually use.

Head to a blank page in your journal and label it "Talent." Bookmark it so that you can find it again later. Draw three rectangles in the center of the page.

Go back to your notes from the exercises in this chapter and put all of your circled talents on the page surrounding the three rectangles. You might want to try grouping similar items together to make it easier to look at.

Then pick the three talents, or areas of talent, that speak most loudly to you and put one in each rectangle. These can be specific or general. These may not be the talents that are repeated most often, these are going to be the talents that you feel most aligned with—the ones that you picture as your superpowers. If you have five talents that really speak to you or only one, go with that.

Feel free to create a few drafts until you feel comfortable with your talents.

Just like your passion, you need to feel these talents in your soul if you want to use them to set a direction toward an exceptional life. And please don't try to quiet your inner voice by choosing the talents you think you "should" pick.

In fact, let's talk about that now.

Waste Your Talent If You Want

We intuitively have a problem with wastefulness. We clean our plates. We turn off the water when we brush our teeth. We give to Goodwill and recycle. And we feel awful about the idea of wasting a perfectly good talent.

But if you choose to use a talent that does not make you happy, you are wasting your joy. And joy is the end goal. Using your talents is part of your journey, not the goal. Talents change! Remember that what you are doing now does not determine what you can do in the future. Look at yourself today. Are you the same person you were a few years ago? Nope.

I am reminded of a little boy in a documentary that I watched called, *First Position*, about young dancers training to compete in a world-renowned ballet competition. One of the dancers had a younger brother who was also entered in the competition. He was quite talented for his age, but he clearly had no desire to use his talent for ballet. Through the movie we watched him not paying attention at rehearsal and hating his itchy, frilly costume and wanting to be doing other things instead of practice. He always looked grumpy. And his mother was focused to the point of obsession about his use of his talent. Luckily, by the end of the movie the little boy had been allowed to waste his ballet talent and take up things that interested him. And finally, we were able to see him as the joyful little boy he was born to be.

But there are some of us who hang onto a talent we hate a little too long.

I was gifted in math. So, when it was time to go to college, my parents wanted to me to be an engineer.

But I was first drawn to dance—I loved it. But I wasn't great at it. But I wanted to learn more. I could happily spend my entire day learning about dance. Maybe I would want to be a dance teacher? Maybe I would have had a breakout moment and become a professional dancer? Maybe I would have found something related to dance to study? But the answer my parents gave me was "no." It was not a secure thing. It was a waste of my talent.

So, my parents continued to push me into engineering. During a campus tour, I was drawn to the hotel management school (my inner-organizer was screaming to come out). I loved food. I loved decorating. I loved entertaining. I loved travel. I could happily spend my entire day learning about working in a hotel. Maybe I would want to be a chef? Maybe I would be an event planner? Maybe I would manage a small B&B in France? But the answer was, "no." Did I want to spend my life serving others? It was a waste of my talent. My parents thought it more exciting to be a girl who excelled at math.

While looking at engineering majors, I was lured in by its cuter sister, architecture. I loved art and buildings. I wasn't a great artist. But I wanted to learn more. I could happily spend my entire day learning about architecture. Maybe I would be an architect? Maybe I would design cool furniture? But the answer was, "no." I was not a good enough artist. It was a waste of my talent.

So, as you may have already guessed, majored in engineering. I studied Operations Research and Industrial Engineering. I can't tell you what I learned because I wasn't interested in learning about it. I did not get good grades because I wasn't interested in the subject matter. I could not get a job in engineering because it bored me.

I ended up in human resources and loved serving others. Then I opened a bakery where I designed cool and crazy cakes. And I volunteered teaching dance to kids. I eventually got to a place where I was doing the things that I liked. But I would have been so much happier and made a bigger impact on the world if I had "wasted my talent" and learned about something that I was interested in to begin with!

So, go ahead. Waste your talent if you want! Because doing what lights up your soul allows you to make an impact on the world.

Discovering your talents has shown you how you can live a life focused on your passion with joy and success.

10.

Impact

"A life is not important except in the impact it has
on other lives."

- Jackie Robinson (baseball player)

There are few things more fulfilling than making the world a
better place.
And when you make an impact in an area you are passionate
about and when you are using your talents, the life you create can be
exceptional.

Our Purpose Is to Improve Humanity

There may be some people reading this book who are hyper-focused
on themselves. People who ask in every decision, "what's in it for
me?" If this is you, I would encourage you to explore this part of
yourself and try to open yourself up to the idea that you are a part of
something greater than yourself and making a positive impact on the
entirety of humanity is part of your reason for being alive.

But regardless of where your head is right now, let's talk about trying to make the world a better place.

Give… No Matter How Small

How do you figure out where you can best impact humanity? It's quite easy. You see something that disturbs you and you want to fix it. And you can simply start by looking at the next person you meet and ask yourself, "How can I make their lives happier?"

And "they" can be millions of people. Or just one. You don't have to solve world hunger to make an impact on humanity. You can buy a homeless man a coffee and a bagel and solve his hunger. Or maybe you are inspired to give a granola bar to every hungry person you meet. Or maybe you start a foundation to feed an entire hungry village. All of those are great things. And all of those made a life happier. All of those were you making an impact. Size doesn't matter.

For most of my adult life, I didn't know where to make an impact. I would watch other people in college organize rallies for one thing or another. When I got older I had coworkers who sat on boards of charitable organizations or started their own. Currently, I watch friends start organizations to save the waterfront or to get guns out of schools. I thought I needed to do something that grand to make a positive impact on the world.

However, I am not a person who desires to lead a service organization. It is not my passion nor where my talents lie. So, for a long time I abstained from helping humanity in any sort of way.

But I was always inspired to help kids live a better life—a life that felt safe and loving and authentic. And lucky for me (and for humanity), I realized a few years ago that I can make an impact on kids' lives in my own way.

My advice to myself became, "See something, Do Something." (Sort of like the Homeland Security campaign "If You See Something, Say Something".) Now when I see a child whose life I could make happier, I do whatever I can. I once knitted an entire box of hats and collected shoes for Syrian refugee children. I volunteer at an organization called the Pajama Program that provides books and jammies to kids in need. I support kids in their love of musical theater by volunteering my time to choreograph the local school musical and coordinate a musical theater program through our arts council. I homeschool my kids. I am writing this book. I sponsor a child through Save the Children. I collect school supplies for Operation Backpack.

I have learned to make an impact in my own special way. One child at a time.

There is a beautiful story I remind myself of whenever I might think that what I am doing doesn't matter because it feels too small.

There was once a young boy walking along a beach that was littered with hundreds of starfish. He picked up every starfish he found and placed it back in the ocean. He was working at this for hours and was barely making a dent. His father came up and said, "Son, there are just too many starfish. You can't possibly make a difference." And his son, with a single starfish in his hand replied, "But I am making a difference to this one."

Sometimes you may do something that seems quite insignificant, but always keep in mind that the littlest thing that you do to make someone's life a little better, may have an impact that you cannot even imagine.

Go to YouTube and watch a commercial for Thai Life Insurance called "Unsung Hero". You will see what I mean.

Every kind thing that you do for another matters. No matter how small.

You Receive by Giving

Why do we strive to make a positive impact on humanity? Why do we strive to make the lives of others better?

One of the reasons is that it makes us feel good. We feel fulfilled and proud and happy. We have done something important. It is not about the approval or thanks that comes back to us. We feel the joy that comes simply from taking action.

If you need a little more convincing, there are scientific studies that prove that giving benefits you.

A study by Michael J. Poulin, PhD at The University of Buffalo found that people who did helpful things for their neighbors and friends—such as running errands, cooking meals, or babysitting—reduced their mortality rates compared with those who did not help.

The Journal of Science found that donating to a charity activates areas of the brain that are also activated by pleasures like eating and sex and a runner's high. When you give you actually FEEL like you received something!

When you give, oxytocin is released into the body. It lowers your stress and makes you feel more connected to others. For up to two hours! According to Scientific American, being stingy, however, releases the stress hormone cortisol into the body.

I actually do an exercise related to this each morning. I have a "giving journal." Every morning I scribble down the ways that I gave the day before. Where I donated money. If I volunteered my time. If I made something for someone. Where I took time out of my day to help someone. When I smiled at someone or let them go in front of me in line. I note all the ways that I gave. I can tell you it makes me feel good and inspires me to do more of the same in the coming day.

And look, some days I find that I didn't give at all and I use that as motivation for the future. A "giving journal" is a great practice for you to try out on your own!

Give. You will receive a whole lot more in return.

Be Aware of How You Impact Humanity

A word of caution to be mindful about what you are actually giving to humanity.

Because you can also make a negative impact on humanity. For some people, it is because you are only thinking about yourself. But for others who strive to make a positive impact, sometimes we don't stop to think how our actions impact others.

Like in the 1960s when people were not aware of what happened when they threw their candy bar wrapper out the car window instead of putting it in a trash can. They weren't intentionally trying to harm humanity and wildlife by dirtying the earth. They weren't thinking. But after the "Keep America Beautiful" ad campaign to educate people, most people realized how they could make a more positive impact and began to put their trash somewhere other than out the car window.

The same idea goes for recycling and child labor and seatbelts. Sometimes we don't know that we are making a negative impact until someone shows us.

And sometimes we know but we get fooled.

We may be concerned with childhood obesity and realize that soda impacts this problem in such an unhealthy way. So of course, we don't buy soda. But we buy cases of water from a soda manufacturer. We don't think about the connection of how our money is going to contribute to impacting society in a negative way. It is probably going towards those commercials where every cute, smiling, singing person has a can of soda in their hand, which is not at all how we wanted to make an impact.

Sometimes the negative impact you are making is minute. But you need to decide, just like with making a positive impact, if you believe that your little actions really do make a difference.

Take the plastic straw for example. According to Jackie Nuñez, founder of *The Last Plastic Straw*, each day more than five hundred million plastic straws are used and discarded in the US alone. These straws are too small to be caught by recycling equipment and end up in our landfills and oceans. Many towns are beginning to outlaw the use of the single-use plastic straw. I have heard a lot of people moan and groan about how we can't possibly improve the planet by getting rid of straws. And you may choose to be okay with the miniscule negative impact you make by using a plastic straw in your grande iced sugar-free soy vanilla latte (say that five times fast). Or, you might decide that any negative impact is too much for you and you can change you habits to use a paper straw or no straw at all. You can hope that if everyone does the same, we will actually make a small dent. You can hope that this small positive impact will put other positive things into play, like the elimination of all single-use plastic, and snowball into a massive positive impact on our planet.

We must think about how each of our actions positively or negatively impact humanity. No matter how small! Because it always starts out small. But it can really add up to make a big impact on humanity.

So Much of Humanity Needs Help

Trying to make an impact may, at times, feel overwhelming.

Sometimes I look around the world and I am paralyzed by the places that need our help. The destruction of our planet. Starving people. Cruelty to animals. Child abuse. Inadequate schooling. Natural disasters. How can I help them all?

I have discovered that I can't.

I am touched by so many things that I read or hear, and I want to help. After a lot of trial and error, I decided that I provide the most help by focusing my efforts on a few of the things that hit me the hardest.

That's not to say that when a friend brings a cause to my attention and needs my help or my donation that I turn them away. If I am touched by it then I help.

But I spend my time actively looking for ways to make an impact only in the areas that I am most concerned about so that I can make the biggest impact possible. I only have so many resources and I believe that the greatest impact comes from not spreading yourself too thin.

Try not to let yourself become so overwhelmed that you become unable to act. Instead take baby steps.

Let me show you a few ways to discover your own unique area of impact.

Explore the Impact You Want to Make

You have a greater purpose on this earth than meeting your own needs. Let's explore how you can make your greatest impact on humanity.

When you do these exercises it is important to put aside "thinking" and really get into "feeling". It is the only way to authentically know what's in your heart.

Who Do You Want to Save?

This exercise motivated me to write this book. It is a simple, yet powerful look at your deepest hurts and your greatest value.

VISUALIZATION: "Little and Big"

Find a quiet space alone with your journal. You are going to do a visualization exercise.

Close your eyes and picture your five-year-old self. Visualize where you are

---

and what you are doing. Watch yourself for a little while. This might feel a bit odd at first but if you let yourself do it and don't give up, I promise it will only take a few minutes for you to start to picture yourself.

Next, tap into the part of your child that doesn't feel appreciated. Let your child-self talk to you. Let them talk about how they feel, what makes them sad, what makes them afraid.

Then, I want you to let your current-self enter the room. I want you to play with the child for a few minutes and then take them up to bed and tuck them in. And say one thing to them.

Write down what you said and then record what you saw, heard, and felt.

Reflect on the experience, especially what you said to your child-self. There is a message in here about who you want to save. When it makes sense to you, write it down, circle it, and label it, "Impact".

"Little and Big" really taps into your subconscious hurts. And wherever you hurt, you'll want to save others from the same hurt.

What Needs Fixing?

There are things in the world that we perceive to be broken. We all notice different things and they point us in the direction of where we want to impact humanity.

EXERCISE: "Something Doesn't Make Sense"

This is a quick exercise. Take out your journal and number a blank page 1 – 50.

Make a list of 50 things that aggravate you or make you sad. Things that make you say, "That's crazy! How can that be happening?" Things that you see in the news or things that happen in your daily life.

Don't think about them, just write them as they pop into your mind.

When you are finished, on a blank page, group together like items. Choose your own categories. Maybe it's the environment or politics or immigration. The categories are your choice. Circle the group that has the most items and label it, "Impact".

"Something Doesn't Make Sense" clues you in to where you feel most motivated to save the world.

Enneagram

The enneagram is a personality typing system that puts people into one of nine types. Once you find your type you are guided to understand the messages you were given as a child and how that has created a belief you carry about yourself. The enneagram type shows you your fears and the responses and unhealthy beliefs you use to protect yourself from those fears. It also helps clue you in on how you want to save the world.

If you want to take an enneagram assessment, *Eclectic Energies* has a great online test and many resources at www.eclecticenergies.com/enneagram/test. If you want to go deeper, I highly recommend the book, *The Wisdom of the Enneagram* by Don Richard Riso.

If you happen to learn a bit about what inspires you from doing some enneagram research, go ahead and circle what you found to be the impact you desire to make and label it, "Impact".

Exploring how you want to positively impact humanity can be eye-opening.

Let's pinpoint exactly where you want to give of yourself toward bettering the world.

Your Impact Discovered

Discovering the change you are driven to make in the world is inspiring. Let's find out what drives you.

Head to a blank page in your journal and label it, "Impact." Bookmark it so that you can find it again later. Draw a circle in the center of the page. Transfer each of the impacts you circled in this chapter's exercises to the page around the circle, so you can see everything together.

The exercises may have all told you the same thing. Or you may need to spend some time thinking about how they all fit together. It may be something incredibly unique. If the impacts you discovered are all different, I might suggest doing the exercises again.

When you feel comfortable with the area you want to impact, write it in the circle.

The impact you discover will be a strong guiding force in setting the direction for an exceptional life. Be sure it speaks to you.

Money Is Not the Motivation

A common worry is that you can't save the world and make money at the same time. But I ask you for a moment to consider that these are two unrelated experiences.

My first job out of college was all about the money and the lifestyle it could afford me. I didn't care what I did, all I cared about was the paycheck. After a few years of working as a computer programmer in the financial industry, I realized that was a rather empty existence for me. I spent some time modifying my beliefs about money so that I could change my job to do something that mattered to me even if it paid less. Something that I felt was valuable to the world.

I moved into Human Resources and was responsible for a small team that managed the staffing of consultants. My new job required me to get to know my consultants and find the best opportunity for them to work on. Something that would help them learn and grow, something they were interested in, and something that met their personal needs. It was perfect for me because it fit nicely into the impact I wanted to make, helping kids live a safe and authentic life. But I made less money. And the increases in pay I could expect were far less than they would have been if I had stayed working as a programmer. But I did it. Because I wanted to make a difference.

And I was great at it. The job not only let me make the impact I wanted but also spoke to my passion for learning and sharing what I had learned and merged with my talent for organization. I was happy to work extra hours. I always went the extra mile. I spent time learning everything I could about the people I supported and the jobs that were available.

My favorite impact I made from this time in my life was when we had a large number of new consultants, fresh from college. A large number of them were sitting around the office unstaffed because their resumés were a little light and they kept getting passed over for other consultants. I worried about them. They were bored, their morale was low, and they were not building any skills. They were falling behind their peers. They were suffering. So, I spent my time getting to know them. I kept my door open to them during the day and I took them out to lunch and dinner a few times. I learned who each really was and what value they could add. And I sold them on specific projects. Each one of them. I called managers I knew and got them to listen to how this particular person would be an asset to their team. I managed to get each of them out the door and on a project. And guess what? They were all huge successes. At the end of the year, they were the highest rated consultants in our office. They were happy, their projects were happy, and our bottom line was happy to have these kids working instead of getting paid to sit around.

And guess who else was happy? Me. Because I was given the top rating in HR that year, a huge salary increase, and a promotion. I was making more money and was more successful than I ever would have been doing something that was only a paycheck.

I realized that whatever you do or create, you have a choice. You can choose to be motivated by money and fame. Or you can choose to be motivated by delivering value and service. You can make money either way. But one is the hard way and one is the easy way.

I am not the only person who is motivated to add value and still makes money. Check out the lives of Uber creators, Travis Kalanick and Garrett Camp who were motivated when they couldn't get a cab one night. Or Elon Musk who created SpaceX to try to save the world. Or media executive Oprah Winfrey who wanted to inspire kids. Or Google founders Larry Page and Sergey Brin who wanted to help people more easily find information on the world wide web. These are people who were motivated to make a positive impact on humanity and made millions (if not billions) of dollars in the process.

Money is important. But don't let it be the reason you make choices in life.

You could easily follow a path determined by only your passion and your talents and do great. Incorporating how you want to help humanity is the driving force to be exceptional because it inspires you to take your life to a whole new level.

11.

Success

"Try not to become a person of success, try rather to become a person of value."

– Albert Einstein (physicist)

Real success happens when you are living to the full potential of your authentic self. It does not matter one bit if you are a doctor, a yogi, a politician, or a street musician. What matters is who you are, not what you are. And that you bring your truest self to your passion, talent, and impact.

Success Is a State of Being

Most of us have been raised in a society that has taught us to believe that success can be measured by what we have acquired in our lives. In this chapter I will challenge you to think differently about success and create your own definition that fits your unique self.

Having Things Does Not Make You Successful

Before I tell you what success is, I want to tell you what it is not. It is not based on any achievements outside of yourself.

Success is not based on a certain number in your bank account. Or a particular car. Or a certain award. Or a ranking in your class. Or a shiny new house. Or expensive shoes. Having these "things" does not make you successful.

Don't get me wrong. "Things" are nice. If you have them because they bring you great joy—cool. Having a car that you baby and polish and enhance and makes you excited to drive down the windy backroads with the top down is a great thing to have. Having a necklace that you thought was the most unique thing in the world and causes you to feel beautiful every time you wear it is a great thing to have. Having a house that you turn into a home for family and friends is a great thing to have.

Things that you have so that other people see them and tell you how great you are, are not great things to have if you have them for this reason. (If you find that you have a lot of things that fall into this category, know that you are not alone! But also know that exploring why you feel that you need these things and the approval of others is something that will serve you well!)

Things can make you happy but they cannot make you successful. Things can be acquired and almost anyone can acquire anything. You can acquire a house because you were "successful," or you could have swindled a lovely old lady out of it. You could have an exotic vacation because you were "successful" or because you tricked your boyfriend into taking you before you dump him. You could have the most coveted jacket of the season because you are "successful" or because you borrowed it from your roommate.

When you are focused on achieving "things" as a signal to yourself that you are successful, you will find that you never have enough. You will constantly need a newer "thing" and a better "thing" to make you feel fulfilled. This is not an exceptional life. This is a life of discontent and constant lacking. In Buddhism, these people get the pleasant name "hungry ghost." They die empty and always wanting more.

Attaching "things" to success also keeps you from following your authentic direction. When you are so focused on achieving a certain symbol of status, you are missing out on the other opportunities that are knocking on your door. Like that time you were so focused trying to catch the eye of the head cheerleader because of her social status that you missed out on a date with the person who would have been your perfect match!

Success is not at all about what you have. It is about something else entirely.

Success Is Character

So, if "having" things does not make you successful, what does?

It is "being." "Being" makes you successful. And I learned this from Ben Franklin.

Benjamin Franklin is well known as one of the founding fathers of the United States of America, as the inventor of bifocals, and that guy with the key and the kite. He was also quite a philosopher and when he was young he identified thirteen characteristics that he felt he needed to be successful in life. He called these the "Thirteen Virtues." Each week he focused on a different characteristic to learn more about it and focus on incorporating it more fully into his life.

Ben's "Thirteen Virtues" were ...

- Temperance. Eat not to dullness; drink not to elevation.
- Silence. Speak not but what may benefit others or yourself; avoid trifling conversation.
- Order. Let all your things have their places; let each part of your business have its time.
- Resolution. Resolve to perform what you ought; perform

without fail what you resolve.

- Frugality. Make no expense but to do good to others or yourself; i.e., waste nothing.
- Industry. Lose no time; be always employ'd in something useful; cut off all unnecessary actions.
- Sincerity. Use no hurtful deceit; think innocently and justly, and, if you speak, speak accordingly.
- Justice. Wrong none by doing injuries, or omitting the benefits that are your duty.
- Moderation. Avoid extremes; forbear resenting injuries so much as you think they deserve.
- Cleanliness. Tolerate no uncleanliness in body, cloaths, or habitation.
- Tranquility. Be not disturbed at trifles, or at accidents common or unavoidable.
- Chastity. Rarely use venery but for health or offspring, never to dullness, weakness, or the injury of your own or another's peace or reputation.
- Humility. Imitate Jesus and Socrates.

Spending some time thinking about this list and the practice of embracing one at a time continually over a lifetime brought me to the realization that success is achieved not by what you "have" over your lifetime, but by how well you achieve "being" in each of the characteristics you deem important.

"Being" fully in a specific characteristic is character.

And success is all about character.

Not everyone finds that the same characteristics speak to them. And that is a beautiful thing because the world would be pretty boring if we were all alike.

The key is to understand what characteristics you would like to focus on in your life.

I like Ben's list a lot but it wasn't quite right for me.

I spent a lot of time thinking about what success looks like to me and came up with my own characteristics...

- Determined
- Observant
- Kind
- Vulnerable
- Joyful

We each need to develop our own list. The list of characteristics that we strive to grow in. The list of characteristics that, when achieved to a considerable degree, will make us feel successful.

Your list will be different from mine and from everyone else's.

Which is why we often find conflict with others. Why we find it hard to work on a team with certain people. Why we become frustrated with our kids. Why we have arguments over politics.

We are all operating with different characteristics in mind. Each of us trying to achieve success in different characteristics.

Nobody is wrong. Only different.

Soon, I am going to have you come up with your own list of characteristics.

But first I want you to shed any characteristics that you think you should have on your list. Because they might not belong to you.

Some Beliefs About Success Are Not Yours

Many of the beliefs you have about success are not your own. They are borrowed from parents and teachers and friends and the media.

Every day of your life people around you are telling you what success looks like. Your parents may think straight A's means success. Your teachers might think it is entry into an Ivy League school. Your friends might think it is being able to buy the latest iPhone. The media may think it is getting over a thousand "likes" on your Instagram selfie.

These may have nothing to do with your idea of success. But you may never even stop to think about that because you have heard these beliefs about success so many times that you think they are your own.

But you have the right and responsibility to decide for yourself what success looks like. You have the right and responsibility to let go of beliefs that no longer serve you.

I am reminded of a story about a man who was passing by a large group of elephants. He stopped suddenly, confused by the fact that these huge animals were being held by only a small rope tied to their front leg. There were no chains or cages. It was obvious to the man that the elephants could break away from the rope and run away at any time. But they didn't.

When the man saw the elephant trainer he asked why the elephants made no attempt to get away. "When they were very young and much smaller," the trainer said, "we used the same size rope to tie them. At that age it was enough to hold them. As they grew up they had become conditioned to believe they could not break away. They believe the rope can still hold them, so they never try to break free."

You may be tied by a rope that held you when you were a child, but I am suggesting that you look down and see that you are no longer bound.

I learned to free myself from beliefs that are not mine from one of my very favorite books, *The Code of the Extraordinary Mind* by Vishen Lakhiani. He calls bad, or unhealthy beliefs "bullshit rules," or Brules.

Vishen says that an "extraordinary mind questions the Brules that are out of alignment with their dreams and desires." These minds "recognize that much of the way the world works is due to people blindly following Brules that have long passed their expiration date."

He does not suggest getting rid of moral and ethical standards but that we should take a good look at beliefs that drag us into "long-held habits and irrational self-judgement" such as "I should call my parents every day or I am not being a good child" or "I should work to the point of exhaustion every week or I'm not working hard enough."

Vishen suggests asking a few thought-provoking questions to test if a belief you hold is a rule you want to live by or a Brule you want to do away with.

1. Is your belief based on trust and hope in humanity? Beliefs that assume that humanity is inherently bad may be Brules.
2. Does your belief violate the Golden Rule? Beliefs that don't support "do unto others" may be Brules.
3. Did you take on your belief from culture or religion? If you are bothered by arbitrary rules about dress, food, or marriage that come from your culture or religion, they may be Brules.
4. Is it based on rational choice or contagion? If you have been following a belief since childhood without question, it may be a Brule.
5. Does it serve my happiness? If a belief does not make you happy, it may be a Brule.

One of the beliefs that I was able to eliminate from my life was something my father had told me as I was picking a major for college and had stayed with me for a long time. I have already mentioned how I went to college and studied engineering.

While on my tour of Cornell, thinking about majoring in something in hospitality, I was dragged swiftly back to reality by my father, who said, "Do you really want to serve others when you could be served?" This was followed by a mini-lecture about how my parents and grandparents and all the way back to great, great, great Uncle Andras in Transylvania had worked serving others. Teachers, city employees, carpenters. Hotel employees.

On the spot, I formed the belief, "Serving others is bad." And my dream changed to one where I was being served.

And I decided to major in engineering so that I could be served by others.

But what I realized many years down the road—that belief did not belong to me. I realized that MY belief is "Serving others is good and important."

The vast majority of us unknowingly take on beliefs that don't belong to us. Beliefs that cause us to treat ourselves or others poorly. I encourage you in the upcoming exercises and in life, that before you allow a belief into your life, about success or anything else, always ask yourself, "Is this belief mine?"

Ready to find out who you want to be when you grow up?

Explore Your Beliefs About Success

Understanding what you believe makes you successful may not set the direction that you take in life as drastically as passion, talent, and impact do, but it is the glue that holds it all together.

As you go through these exercises, remember, there are no right answers. Only your answers.

This Means Success

Sometimes we are a little unclear about what could be considered a characteristic of success because we are so used to thinking in terms of "things."

Sometimes a little list can help!

You may just find your character from this exercise alone.

EXERCISE: "Success List"

This exercise is simple. You are going to pick the characteristics that you want to "be."

Go through the list on the following pages and either circle the items in this book or write them in a list in your journal.

You will probably look at almost every characteristic on the list and think they are worthy of being circled, but I want you to pick the ones that are most important to you. Probably around 25. So, when you want to circle one, I want you to think about living life without that characteristic. Could you be happy? If so, you probably don't want to circle it. Or at least make a note that it is not on your "must have" list.

abundant
accepting
accomplished
active
adaptable
adored
affectionate
aggressive
agile
alert
always learning
ambitious
amusing
appreciated
appreciative
approachable
articulate
attention to detail
attentive
aware
balanced
benevolent
bold
brave
brilliant
calm
candid
careful
caring
challenging
charismatic
charitable
charming
cheerful
clean
clear
clever
committed
communicative
competitive
complimentary
confident
connected
contributing
cool
cordial
correct
courageous
creative
credible
curious
decisive
dependable
detached
determined
devoted

diligent
direct
disciplined
discrete
diverse
dominating
dreamy
driven
dynamic
educated
effective
efficient
emotional
energetic
experienced
exploring
fair
fascinated by life
fearless
ferocious
firm
flexible
focused
forgiving
forward-moving
friendly
frank
frugal
fun-loving
generous
goes above-and-beyond
graceful
grateful
growth-oriented
happy
helpful
honest
humble
independent
industrious
inspired
intelligent
intense
intuitive
inventive
joyful
just
kind
knowledgeable
leader
listener
logical
magnetic
mature

mellow
meticulous
mindful
noticing
obedient
observant
open
open-minded
optimistic
organized
outlandish
passionate
patient
peaceful
perceptive
playful
poised
popular
positive
practical
prepared
present
proactive
professional
questioning
quiet
relationship builder
relaxed
resilient
resourceful
seeking equality
self-assurance
self-reliant
sense of humor
shrewd
silent
sincere
smiling
solution-oriented
speedy
strategic
strong
structured
sympathetic
team player
tenacious
tolerant
trustworthy
uncomplaining
understanding
unique
vulnerable
warm
willing
wise

Once you have picked the characteristics that speak to you, see if you can group like ones together and then pick the 5 most important groups or words to you. Write them on a blank page, circle them, and label them, "Success".

"Success List" can open your mind to what success can really look like for you.

Success is Right Before Your Eyes

You already know what success means to you. Because you are inspired every day by people who are living the way you want to. You are inspired by people who care about others. By people who take risks. By people who work hard. By people who are happy.

They hold the key to unlocking what you believe about success and about who you want to be.

EXERCISE: "Looking Up. And Down."

You are going to explore some of the people that inspire you. And don't.

On a blank page in your journal, split the page into two columns. Put the number "1" on the first line in the first column. Skip two lines, then repeat with "2" through "10", skipping two lines after each number.

Think of ten people you really admire. People who you view as "successful." They can be people you know or people you see in the media. Think through family members, friends, teachers, people in your community. Think through your favorite celebrities. Put each of their names in the first column after the number.

Then take a few minutes to list three characteristics you really admire for each person in the second column.

Now I want you to set up another page the same way, except with three columns.

Think of ten people who you do not admire. People who you would not call "successful." Again, they can be people you know or people you know of. Put their names in the first column.

After you have your list, take a few minutes to list three characteristics that you do not admire for each person in the second column. When you are done,

---

write the opposite of that characteristic in the third column. The third column holds the characteristics you would actually admire.

On a blank page, rewrite every characteristic you admired. Repeats are fine. Group similar characteristics together. Circle the five groups that have the most items or that feel the most important to you. Label them "Success".

"Looking Up. And Down" clearly shows you what success looks like to you.

Let me help you make some sense of what you uncovered.

Your Beliefs About Success Discovered

The success exercises are usually the ones that really speak to people. The exercises make it crystal clear on what success means to you.

Now, head to a blank page in your journal and label it, "Success". Bookmark it so that you can find it again later. Draw five circles in the center of the page. Transfer all of your "Successes" from this chapter's exercises to around the circles, grouping similar items together. Pick the five success characteristics that stand out to you and write them in the circles.

Close your eyes for a minute and picture yourself twenty years from now fully embodying these characteristics. Do you feel content? Do you feel successful? If so, you have picked characteristics that are aligned with your authentic self. If not, go back and look at your lists from your exercises and replace some characteristics until your visualization feels just right. And remember, your characteristics are your choices, not someone else's.

Feel free to have a few more characteristics on your "Success" page if that feels right to you.

No matter what passion, talent, or impact you embrace, living a life in alignment with your chosen characteristics will make you feel like a success in everything you do.

12.

Happiness

"Happiness is not something you postpone for the
future. It is something you design for the
present."

- Jim Rohn (philosopher)

Happiness is not a "nice to have." It is an essential part of your
authentic self and must be embraced in order to live an exceptional
life.

Happiness is Essential

There is a misunderstanding amongst most of civilized society. That
being happy all the time is selfish.

Far too many people believe that happiness can wait. That you can
wait to be happy until the bills have been paid, until the report has
been written, until you have retired. But happiness cannot wait. It is
an integral part of who you are and without it, all the other parts of
your life will suffer. And that includes everyone you touch.

Being happy is not being selfish! It is essential!

Happiness Raises Your Vibration

At every given moment, every being on the planet is vibrating. Some are vibrating at a low frequency and some are vibrating at a high frequency. Every person on this planet has a vibration. Some of us vibrate really high in a space of love and joy and peace. And other people are in the lower vibrations of fear and anger and shame.

The emotional guidance scale by Abraham-Hicks illustrates all of the levels of vibration. Joy, passion, enthusiasm, optimism, hopefulness, and contentment are examples of high vibration emotions. Doubt, worry, anger, jealousy, guilt, and fear are lower vibration emotions.

When you are vibrating at a lower frequency, you experience physical pain and discomfort, heavy emotions, and darker energy. It takes a great deal of effort to accomplish the things you want to. Your life has a generally negative feel to it.

When you are vibrating at a higher frequency, you are healthy, full of personal power, and have clarity and peace. You more easily attract the things you want in your life. Your life tends to gravitate towards the exceptional.

Doing things that make you happy is one great way to increase your vibration. Involving yourself with your passion every day, making a difference in the lives of others, and being the kind of person you aspire to be are also going to raise your vibration. But don't discount the importance on the vibration of filling your life with the simple pleasures that make you happy.

Think back to a period of time when you were too busy to do the things that make you happy. Perhaps when you had too much homework and studying and you couldn't see your friends or make it to sports practice or even get enough sleep. Can you remember getting sick? Or being cranky? Or depressed? I bet you can.

Making room in our lives for the things that make us happy is essential to a higher vibration. And a higher vibration is essential to an exceptional life.

Happiness is Contagious

Have you ever been in a bad or low mood and walked into a room full of happy people? You can't help but have your mood lifted.

That's because happiness begets happiness.

People are like tuning forks. We pick up the vibration of people who are near us and we begin to vibrate like them.

I had a good friend, but we recently had to break up because she was trashing my vibration!

I have to admit that Sue has always been a little negative—and for a while, so was I. Our greatest bond was our desire to complain about an organization we were both part of. We enjoyed discussing how disorganized it was and how it lacked talent and how it was so outdated (I know...why were we still there?!). We were both vibrating lower than average around worry and discouragement. We fed off each other and we kept each other in that low vibration when we were together.

But then something happened in the organization that made Sue horribly angry. Her vibration dropped into revenge and rage. It became physically painful for me to be around her. To counteract her really low vibration, I went higher. I worked on my issues and I rose to a place where I could feel content and hopeful about the organization and when we were together I tried to maintain that vibration. But an extremely low vibration has a strong pull (as does an extremely high vibration) and time after time I found myself fighting to not be dragged down. It was draining. And after a few months I decided to gracefully wish her well and move on.

Now, when I am involved with the organization, I am still not able to be in a high vibration. And that is a sign for me to move on to a place where I can be vibrating in enthusiasm and joy. But at least

I am in an upward spiral and making the effort to find people and organizations who raise my vibration, not lower it.

Being happy is a high vibration. Which is not only good for you, but for everyone you come in contact with.

Make time for your happiness. You can't have an exceptional life without it!

Explore What Makes You Happy

If you don't fill your day with things that make you happy, it doesn't matter how much or your passion or talent you are using. If you don't fill your day with things that make you happy, it doesn't matter what kind of impact you are making on the world or if you are being the kind of person you are proud of. Without happiness all of the rest is dull and a life can never be truly exceptional.

Let's find your happy place.

How Do You Truly Want to Spend Your Time?

One of the easiest ways to discover what makes you happy is to think about what you would want to do with your time if you only had a limited amount left on this earth.

Let's pretend for a moment.

EXERCISE: "Last Month on Earth"

Grab your journal and get ready to imagine your last month on earth.

Close your eyes and get yourself into the mindset of having found out that you only have a month left on Earth. Feel free to create whatever scenario you

---

need to get into this exercise. It might be illness or the end of the world or moving to a remote village in Tibet for ten years. But think about the people and things you will be leaving behind.

From this space, make a list in your journal of 25 things you would want to do before your departure.

Don't judge yourself for putting down silly or frivolous things. Put down whatever you want to do with that time. It could be a favorite meal or spending time with a certain someone or reading a book that you have always put off or hiking a tall mountain or spending lots of time in bed watching TV.

When you have your list of 25, go back over it and remove anything that was really "should." Like cleaning your house. You might want to leave a clean house for your loved ones or spend an afternoon with Great Aunt Janet but that is not truly how you want to spend your time. So, pretend I will gift you these "shoulds" and cross those items off and replace them with a "want."

Next, try putting your to-dos together into groups of similar items like "reading" or "being with people" or "spending time in nature." It is perfectly fine to have no groups and only single items for this one!

"Last Month on Earth" helps you to realize what makes you happiest.

What Catches Your Eye?

This is a fun exercise for the artist in all of us to see what makes us feel great.

You can use a large poster board for this exercise or go digital!

ART PROJECT: "Inspiration Collage"

Grab a pile of magazines (at least three) and your poster board. We are going to make a collage!

Flip through the pages of the magazines pulling out pictures or words that make you feel happy. Clip them out and arrange like items together. Then either glue the pictures to the poster board, or take photos of them on your phone and put them into a digital collage, keeping the groups together.

"Inspiration Collage" is a great way to let your subconscious guide you to remembering what makes you happy.

What Do You Want?

Deep down inside, you know what you want and how you like to spend your time. Now you get to write about it and bring it front and center.

FREE WRITING: "I Want"

Free writing is a wonderful way to bypass your thinking brain and get to the truth that is lingering in your heart.

Grab your journal and a quiet place and then write three full pages without stopping. Your topic is "I Want." Go!

You might want to look a certain way or create something or spend time with certain people. You might want to go places or be alone or cook a meal. You might want new clothes or a relationship or to learn something. Keep writing "I want…." Feel free to elaborate on some of your wants or you can keep moving from one to the next.

When you are done, go back through your writing and on a separate page in your journal start recording the things you want, grouping similar items together if you have them.

"I Want" helps you to see what makes you happy—without giving you time to judge!

You have a long list of what makes you happy. Let's learn how to use it.

Your Unique Happy Place Discovered

Finding your happy place is easy!

Head to a new page in your journal and write down EVERYTHING you discovered in the exercises in this chapter. You can eliminate any repeats or merge together things that feel similar, but you want to capture everything, not only the most popular answers like in the previous chapters.

Then go through your list and think about not doing a particular thing ever again. Do you really care? There may be some things that make you happy but living without them would not make you unhappy. You can cross these off. They are nice, but not essential to your happiness.

Next, grab a new page and label it, "Happiness" and divide it into, "Daily," "Often," and "Yearly." Go through each item and think about doing it. Do you feel like you need to do it daily to be happy? Like running or having coffee? Then put it in the, "Daily," list. If you think about an item and feel like you could be happy doing it every week or month or so then put it in the, "Often," list. These might be things like having dinner with your sister or spending a whole day reading. And if you think about an item and it feels like a once a year thing, like a vacation, then put it in the, "Yearly," list.

If anything on your list is something that is so ingrained in your life and so easy for you to do that you don't even have to think about it, then put a star next to it. If taking a shower every night or a cup of tea in the morning or slipping into cozy pajamas makes you happy and it happens no matter how busy you are or where you are or who you are with, then put a star next to it. This is already part of you and no matter what, you make it happen.

Having a crystal clear idea of what you need to be happy is great. Because you know that happiness is essential to living your best life.

13.

Your Authentic Self

"Cultivate your confidence. Grow your power.
Become the amazing gift that you are to yourself
and share it with the world."

- Christie Marie Sheldon (energy healer)

Here it is. The moment you've been waiting for. The moment that you visualize your authentic self. (I am so excited for you!)

Be True to You

Before we take everything you learned about yourself and put it together into a tool you can use to guide yourself through life, I want to give you a few suggestions for getting the most out of all the hard work you just put in.

Be Honest

Please resist the urge to fit all of your answers to the exercises to some preconceived notion of what you "should" be doing.

The only person who will ever see your picture of your authentic self is you. And you can choose to use it, or you can choose to toss it aside. But please give yourself the chance to see what is in your heart and soul.

You may not be ready to align your actions with it right now, but maybe someday. And doing the exercises with complete honesty will at least provide you with some information that may be a spark that someday starts to smolder.

These exercises are only for you and for your greatest benefit, so be truthful with yourself!

Be Creative

Discovering your authentic self is more an art than a science, more like putting paint to paper than following directions in a lab. It is a process that is unique to each person.

I can guide you through the steps to using what you have learned to paint a picture of your authentic self, but I cannot give you a workbook or a multiple choice test. There are no right answers. Just the right answers for you.

I encourage you to think outside the box to see how your passion, talent, desired impact, beliefs about success, and happiness all fit together into your authentic self. Don't be afraid to take an unconventional route.

These exercises are to guide you. But please feel free to use whatever methods you need to discover what lights you up.

Be Balanced

I encourage you to create a balance between your passion, talent, desired impact, beliefs about success, and happiness.

If you focus too heavily on one area of your life you will find yourself unbalanced. Keeping in balance will lead to greater joy, which will then lead you to live an exceptional life. When we are involved with what we love (passion and happiness) and doing our best to make a difference in the world (talent and impact) and being our greatest version of ourselves (success)—we are creating the greatest joy for ourselves and others. And that is, at the simplest level, our purpose in life. To have joy.

When we are too focused on one area, we begin to feel we are lacking in other areas of our life. People who are so focused on creating joy for themselves, often lack a sense of purpose greater than themselves. And while they are off having a great time and living life, they are likely feeling rather empty because their existence on this planet is making no difference. And people who are too focused on creating joy for others, often lack a sense of self-love. While they are off saving the world, they feel a sense of emptiness because they are not doing anything to restore and rejuvenate themselves.

Too much of a good thing can be a bad thing!

When working through these exercises, I encourage you to treat all of the information you have discovered about yourself with equal importance.

Be Excited

When you discover your authentic self, it is my hope that you feel excited.

I want the picture you visualize to resonate with you so much that it makes you jump out of bed in the morning.

If it doesn't, it is not your authentic self, and you might want to work through some of the exercises again until you are looking upon a self that makes your stomach flutter and your heart beat faster and your skin tingle. Almost a feeling like being in love. Because when you see your authentic self, you can't help but fall head-over-heels in love with it.

Being so in love with your authentic self makes the rest of the book easy to follow. Because it makes the rest of your life a life of ease.

But following a picture of a person who is not your authentic self will be hard work and will set you up for a mediocre life.

So be sure you are excited by what you discover! (And by the way, it's okay to be a little scared! We will cover that later.)

I invite you keep these suggestions in mind while you are working through the exercises in this chapter.

Ready or not, here we go!

Discovering Your Authentic Self

After exploring who you are through the exercises in the past five chapters, you probably already have a much better idea of your truest self. And that is exactly what you need to know in order to live an exceptional life.

But right now, all of the information is sort of floating around in your head and in your journal. Which makes it hard to use to guide yourself toward an exceptional life.

This section will help you to take that information and refine it, put it all together, and find a way to present it to yourself in a way where you can use it as a guiding light in your life.

What is Your Passion, Really?

The first step in putting everything together to become your authentic self is to refine your passion.

You spent a great deal of time discovering your passion back in Chapter 8. So, you know what you like doing. But why do you like it? You need to think deeply.

If you love soccer, was it that you loved being outdoors? Or scoring a goal? Or being part of a winning team? Or practice? Or those cool shoes? All of the above?

If you love bonsai tree sculpting, is it looking for a new design? Or buying the perfect little tree? Or the pruning? Or giving the pruned tree as a gift? All of the above?

If you love video games, is it the graphics? Or the story? Or the competition?

You have to go deep into your passion because there are certain parts of your passion that you love and certain parts that you could live without, or even dislike. It is important to know which parts are which.

For example, loving animals can steer you to becoming a veterinarian or steer you to becoming a dog walker or a pet shop owner or a shelter worker. It all depends on what you love about animals.

That is why you have to dig deep here.

I made the mistake of thinking that my passion was baking. I even opened a bakery. Then it drained the life out of me and I sold the company.

I loved opening the bakery. I loved planning my menu and building my website and constructing the space. I loved meeting with clients to plan out their cakes and scheduling out what would have to get done. I loved creating software to track my orders and inventory. And I loved the challenge of planning and sketching a unique cake (like a three-foot-tall replica of the Miami Hurricanes mascot with a massive beak and standing on one foot).

I did not love making the cakes. I certainly found no joy in mixing and baking. It was boring and messy. I liked the decorating part, but it was stressful because I was always worried that things were going to fall apart.

And I hated the result—the moment where I waited to see if someone liked what I had created.

So, in hindsight, my passion was the preparation phase of baking and I would have been living a far more exceptional life if I had opened a bakery with someone whose passion was the baking, decorating, and delivering so that I could have focused on the part I was truly passionate about.

Let's revisit your passion for a bit so you can avoid my mistake!

EXERCISE: "The Process of Passion"

Grab the page from your journal that you bookmarked as, "Passion," and remind yourself what you put in that big circle. Then, head to a blank page, label it "Real Passion" and bookmark it. Write your passion at the top of a new page in your journal. Then make three columns: "Prep," "Do," "Result." This is the "process of passion."

Close your eyes and spend some time imagining yourself involved in your passion.

Think about the Preparation. What sorts of things do you do before you start? If your passion was painting houses, the prep part would be taping, sanding walls, covering up the floors.

Think about Doing. What is the main part of your passion? Like actually painting the walls. Or more detailed, painting around windows and doors, painting the bulk of the walls, painting the trim and woodwork.

Think about the Result. What happens when you have completed the doing? A beautiful, freshly painted room. A happy customer. A paycheck.

Make some notes about these parts of the process of your passion.

Then think about variations to the process. Are you alone or with others. What is it like when the weather is hot or cold? How does it feel if the project is incredibly difficult or easy-as-pie.

Make some changes to your notes like changing, "painting trim," to "painting complex trim," and "painting easy trim," if these actually feel different to you.

Now go through your parts of the process and cross off any parts or variations that you truly don't love. The ones that you really want to live without. If there are things that you cannot tolerate, they are not part of your passion and doing them is going to take a toll on your exceptional life.

Note: There will be times in your life that you do things that you don't like, because it is an unavoidable part of something you do love. For example, you may love medicine, but you hate doing paperwork. You may end up having to do paperwork if you decided that your path leads you to becoming a doctor. But these things should not be part of your guidance system. By narrowing down the things you like about medicine to diagnosis and interacting with patients, you might find a fit somewhere that does not even involve paperwork!

Lastly, put a big circle at the bottom of the page. You are going to enter your true passion here.

Take a good look at which parts are not crossed off of your list.

If you really didn't cross anything off, then I would say your passion stays the same as the one you started with. So, put that in the new square.

If you crossed off most of the parts in "Prep," "Do," or "Result," then you will want to refine your passion to be more specific to the phase or phases of the process that have nearly all of their items. Liking the Prep phase of your passion but maybe not the Do phase will lead you in a much different direction than if you like the Do and Result and not the Prep. Put your refined passion in the new square.

If your parts are scattered among the three phases, then you will need to spend some time looking for a way to define your new passion. Feel free to be wordy at this point! Or make a little list. You may refine it further in the next exercise. Once you have it defined in a way you feel comfortable using, put it in the new circle.

The, "Process of Passion," exercise is essential. I know it is challenging and a lot of work, but it keeps you focused on what you are truly passionate about, not just a general area.

Who Are You?

Here is where we put together everything you learned about yourself on one sheet of paper.

Your passion, talent, and impact come together to point you in the direction of what you want to do with your life. They show you where you want to learn and work and volunteer. Where and how you want to grow and give.

Your beliefs about success show you what you need to feel fulfilled and your happiness shows you what you need to recharge yourself.

They all come together to form your authentic self, and when realized, bring you an exceptional life of joy.

EXERCISE: "A Map of Self"

Grab the bookmarked pages in your journal labeled, "Real Passion,"Talent," "Impact," "Success," and "Happiness."

Find a blank page, turn it to landscape and label it, "Authentic Self."

Draw a circle in the middle of the page and enter your passion.

Draw three circles above your passion and fill in your talents.

Draw a circle under your passion and write in your desired impact.

To the left of the shapes, list your characteristics for success.

To the right of the shapes, write as many of the things that make you happy as you would like. I would suggest picking the most important things and also leaving the starred items off this page to make the information easier to look at.

Congratulations, you have a rough draft of your authentic self.

Try It on For Size

Once you have a draft of your authentic self, you need to try it on to see if it feels right. That way you know if it is yours.

Allow yourself to dig in to this, you may be surprised what you find out about yourself.

VISUALIZATION: "Dream"

Set aside an hour and find a quiet place. Take your draft of your authentic self and your journal with you.

Close your eyes. I want you to dream. You can either sit and dream or do this as more of a journaling exercise.

This may feel a little silly in the beginning but given a few minutes of being allowed to dream, I always find that I become so immersed into the scenario I create that I can see it and feel it and taste it like I was there.

Picture yourself diving into your passion. Maybe you're in school learning about it or in a job that fulfills your passion. No restrictions here! It can be a totally made up college major or job or experience. Try a few different ideas on for size.

Then work your talent into what you are doing. Fine tune what you are learning or doing to focus on using and building your superpowers. Play around with how this fits into your passion. Be creative. Keep dreaming.

Next, put your talent and passion to great use by bringing them to where you want to make an impact. Use them to make a difference in the world. Try on big ideas and small ones. See how they feel. Where is the sweet spot?

Now picture yourself embodying the characteristics that will make you successful. See yourself being there. Feel it.

Sprinkle your dream with the things that make you happy. Make sure you can do them as you need to, that your dream does not conflict with them.

After a few minutes you will get a feel for this—perhaps even enjoy it! Keep dreaming. Continue playing around until you have a picture of yourself that lights you up inside. Take some notes. Write a ton in your journal, if you want.

Then revise your authentic self to capture what you learned. Note any nuances that were important to you. Remove anything that didn't feel right or didn't matter to you.

Feel good about it before we move on to create a way for you to use this as your compass.

Being crystal clear on your authentic self is an incredible accomplishment.

Next, we are going to put your authentic self into a tool that can guide you every day.

Remember Who You Are

What an accomplishment! You have discovered your authentic self!

But what you discovered about your authentic self won't be helpful if you don't use it. Our next step is to create a tool to remind you of your authentic self every day.

But first, I want to mention something about your authentic self.

Your authentic self may have appeared as something specific. Your passion for the human body, your talent for entertaining kids, and your desire to impact countries with poor health care, paired with happiness that comes from meeting new people, debating, reading, and traveling, and the idea that success means being well-educated, confident, decisive, and creative may have you dreaming about studying pediatric medicine at Yale and then working with Doctors Without Borders. Your authentic self is quite specific.

Or it may be more general. Your passion for Broadway musicals, your talent for entertaining, and your desire to impact people by making each person's day a little happier, paired with happiness that come from city life, staying up late, and traveling, and the idea that success means being friendly, honest, and hardworking may lead you to pursue a dream of acting in New York City. But you might want to try some acting classes and do background work and go on auditions. You might want to teach some acting classes. You might want to work as a performer on a cruise ship. You haven't pictured your five-year plan. Which is actually even better! You are open to lots of different opportunities. You are not limiting yourself. Your authentic self is open to many opportunities.

Wherever you are right now, it is handy to distill your authentic self into a clear vision you can refer to every day and in every moment.

A clear vision helps keep you from getting distracted by all of the un-truths that want to derail you. A clear vision helps you to become what you envision and resolve your internal conflicts.

I have several suggestions that you can use to create a vision for yourself. Pick the one that resonates with you. Or try a few until you figure out which one works best for you. Or create your own.

- Write a one-page story about what your authentic life looks like. Read it every morning or when you are in the middle of a big life change or making a decision.
- Create a list of the traits of your authentic self. Put it as a reminder in your phone and have it pop up at least once a day or turn it into a piece of art that hangs on your wall.
- Turn your list into a few words and have them stamped onto a bracelet or necklace that you wear.
- Write a one or two sentence personal mission statement. Memorize it and repeat it to yourself each day.
- Create an inspiration board with photos that represent your authentic self. Hang it in your room where you can see it every day or use it as the background on your computer or phone.
- Pretty up your "Map of Self" (online or on paper) and leave room for notes. Print out a new copy each week. Throughout the week note the ways that you have aligned with the different aspects of your authentic self.
- Write a poem about your authentic life. Read it each night before bed.

Having this tool is essential to making decisions and keeping you motivated in education, career, and life that are aligned with your authentic self and allow you to live an exceptional life.

Create a method of visualizing your authentic self every day that works for you. And always remember the words of the great writer and philosopher, Ralph Waldo Emerson, "To be yourself in a world that is constantly trying to make you something else is a great accomplishment."

There Is One More Aspect Of Your Authentic Self

Each of us has a reason we are here on this earth. We each have a soul purpose.

Your soul purpose is not something you can do, like being a doctor or being confident or traveling the world. It is the way in which you transform the world no matter what you do, like helping transform darkness into light or being a guide.

As you progress through your journey of life your soul purpose will begin to reveal itself more and more and you will find that it adds a glittering layer to your already exceptional authentic self.

And it is too complex to cover in this book! Because your soul purpose isn't really something that you can discover after a few exercises, it something you will uncover little by little over the course of your life. There are books and courses that can help, but it is a very an organic process.

You may wonder why I am telling you that you have a soul purpose if I am not going to help you find it. It is because I want you to be aware that it exists and, when you begin to discover it, know that it does not negate everything you have learned here about your authentic self, it is just an added bonus.

So have no fear that you have not fully uncovered your soul purpose. It will come to you as it is meant to and will make your authentic self shine even brighter!

Your authentic self is the foundation for your exceptional life.

Now let's find out how you are going to use it to guide your journey.

PART IV

FOLLOW YOUR OWN UNIQUE DIRECTION

Congratulations on discovering your authentic self. That amount of awareness alone is big step toward changing your life!

The next step on your journey to an exceptional life is to set a direction that is aligned with your authentic self. We will discuss where and how to focus your energy each day. You will learn how to deal with opportunities and challenges that life throws you. I encourage you to embrace change as part of your direction. We will tackle the wide world of education. And I'll help you to talk through your unique direction with your parents or closest support system.

14.

It's the Journey, Not the Destination

"Trust the wait. Embrace the uncertainty. Enjoy the beauty of becoming. When nothing is certain, anything is possible."

- Mandy Hale (blogger)

You don't have to wait to start living in alignment with your authentic self until you reach some destination you have in mind or because you think you know what will take you to that destination. Do what feeds your authentic self, in every moment. Time is not a given. Start living now!

A Journey Is Made Up of Small Steps

You are in control of what you put into your every day. Every little thing.

Contribute Each Day

If you want to live an exceptional life, add things to your day that light up your authentic self. Right away. Because an exceptional life does not happen when you reach an end goal. It happens when you live each and every day as your authentic self.

If your authentic self is passionate about computer programming, then be a computer programmer. Today.

Don't wait to be a programmer until you have gotten a job with a software company. Or you have a degree in comp sci. Or until you can program an award-winning game that rivals Fortnite.

Start being a programmer right away—in mind, body, and soul!

Believe you are a programmer and behave like a programmer.

Write programs. Play around with games and apps. Learn new programming languages. Take classes. Volunteer to program for a nonprofit or for friends.

Do those things and you are taking the journey of a programmer.

Some of the actions you take will support the whole of your authentic self. But some will be most focused on helping you move forward in your passion or perhaps cultivate your talent. It is perfectly fine for the focus of an action to be one single part of your authentic self. The only thing that is not okay, is if it goes against other parts of your authentic self. For example if your passion is cooking and one of the things that makes you happy is living in a big city, you might not consider taking a position as a sous chef in a remote village in Mongolia (although that does sound kinda cool). Don't sacrifice one part of your authentic self for another. Remember the balance!

For me, writing this book is aligned with my authentic self of being a guide. Every day I set aside time in the morning for thinking and planning. I try to take a walk every day to reflect on some ideas. I try to read a few articles or blog posts each day. Every week I schedule in at least ten hours to write parts of my book or my blog. When I have time, I work on formatting the book and brainstorm about ways to get my message out to the young adults who are ready to hear it. Every day I am being a guide in some form. Some days what I do is significant, like filming an online workshop and I feel like a true guide. And other days it is something seemingly small, like posting a quote on Instagram, but with that action I am still living as a guide. Some days I do something that impacts others, like writing a blog post. And other days I do something that feeds me internally like reading an article. I need continuing education and I also need to recharge—I'm not good as a guide for others if I'm not my healthiest self. Some days I act like an experienced guide by suggesting a helpful book to someone. And sometimes I am a student watching a video of the Dalai Lama talking about authenticity. No matter the size or shape of what I am doing, I am contributing to my authentic self every day.

Do something every day that puts you in alignment with your authentic self. It does not matter how small or simple. The key is to keep moving in your unique direction.

Let's come up with a few ideas now.

Take Action

Every day. Every week. Every year. You can do things that move you in the direction of your unique self.

EXERCISE: "Bucket List"

Pull out your journal and the reminder of your authentic self.

Brainstorm ideas for how you can contribute to the growth of your authentic self. Come up with at least twenty-five ideas. Nothing is too big or outlandish! Money, time, and the scope of your experience are no object. Your ideas can truly exist or maybe they only exist in your imagination right now.

Now, I want you to pick something you can do every day and start doing it today.

Then, I want you to pick something thing you can do every week and schedule it.

Next, I want you to pick one item you can do this month and schedule it.

Lastly, I want you to pick one thing off the list that you can do this year and plan that out.

Keep the rest of the list somewhere where you can refer back to it. Consider it a bucket list. As you accomplish things, pick new ones to work on. And when you have new ideas of how you can contribute to the growth of your authentic self, add them to your list.

"Bucket List" helps you make a contribution to your authentic self every day. And that is going to serve you well in life!

Set off in your own direction. Right now. No matter how small the step.

There Is More Than One Right Way

If there is one thing you can take away from this book, let it be that there is more than one way to get where you are going.

There Are No Guarantees

You can take a route filled with whimsical, magical, beautiful things to see and do. Or you can take a desolate freeway. You are going to arrive at your destination either way.

And you have no idea which will end up being the shorter or faster route, but you can pretty well guess which one will be more enjoyable!

My point? Please don't fill your journey with activities and experiences you don't enjoy in hopes that they will deliver you to your desired destination. Do not throw away your present for an unknown, hypothetical future.

It goes back to that balance thing. Don't sacrifice your happiness only to misuse your talent or forsake your passion to be a "success." Because you have absolutely no idea if sacrificing your passion or talent will even matter.

We have a family friend, Madison, who is a junior in high school. She is incredibly smart, attending an elite technology high school. She is super involved with her community, working closely with the youth group at her church. She has lots of extracurriculars, including dancing and playing the harp. But the thing she loves most of all is her summer camp.

Madison goes to a good old-fashioned summer camp for one month each summer. She practices archery, goes hiking, and builds campfires. She sleeps in a cabin, makes friendship bracelets, and has color wars. And for the eleven months of the year that Madison is not in camp, she talks about camp. First, she talks about what she did at camp and the people at camp and the food at camp and the interesting bugs at camp. Then as we get close to the time of year she heads back to camp; the conversation turns to her excitement about what will happen at camp in the coming year and who will be there and what cabin she will be in and what activities she will sign up for.

This year, as Madison was telling me all about camp, she also told me she was sad she wouldn't be going back as a counselor next year. I was surprised. She had been looking forward to being a counselor and I could not imagine her not back at camp.

What could have happened to cause this decision? Did the camp close? Was she ill? Was there a terrible financial problem? Nope. She told me she needed to spend her summer time on things that would look good on a college application. Like a summer debate club.

I was so disheartened by her decision. Madison didn't have a magical crystal ball. that told her that "camp counselor" was going to look worse to the college of her choice than the summer debate team. She, and her parents and teachers, had no idea. She could spend an entire summer being unhappy only to end up in the same place she would have gotten to if she had done what she loved.

By doing what she loves as a camp counselor, Madison will most likely make more of an impact. The kid whose life she touches by helping them get over their fear of sleeping away from home just might have a thankful parent who is an alumnus from her preferred school and will call the president and sing her praises. Or the debate team may have a new director and lose its best debater and get crushed at every debate leaving Madison with a dismal experience to put on her record.

You have no idea what action is going to be the best to move you forward. So, pick the one that lights you up inside and then do your very best at it. Remember how we talked about how much brighter you shine when you are doing something you are passionate about?

You Decide What Your Journey Looks Like

Let's talk about the word "should." I would love to eliminate it from everyone's vocabulary.

There are things that you "want" to do. Great! Do them!

And there are things, like doing your laundry so that your socks don't walk away on their own, that you do not want to do but are "required to do." You can do them yourself or find someone to do them for you or find an alternative option.

But things that you "should" do are things that you don't want to do and are not required to do, but you feel pressured to do. There are no "shoulds" in an exceptional life.

"Shoulds" keep you trapped in a direction that is not your own. They are also a key source to feeling angry!

EXERCISE: "Eliminate the Shoulds"

Grab your journal and find a quiet spot.

On a blank page, create four columns. Label them "Want," "Required," and "Should." Leave the last one blank.

Now work backward through your past week. Everything you did goes into one of the three columns. Include assignments from work or school, get-togethers with friends, time you spent alone, chores, appointments, and anything else that you spent a decent amount of time on last week.

Once you have filled up your columns, I want you to take a good look at them.

For the "Required" column, I encourage you to explore how you might get out of this requirement. Is it really required or is it actually a "Should?" Can you substitute something you want to do for it? Can you find a way to turn it into a want? Can you delegate it? While it is not always possible, try to remove the "Required" items from your life since they don't align with your authentic self. There should really be very few of these if you are making choices aligned with your authentic self.

Now for the "Shoulds." Label the last column, "Can." Spend time understanding what you think you are going to get from doing this "Should." Then cross it off and in the "Can" column write down something that you can do instead that will give you what you think the "Should" is but is in alignment with your authentic self. For example, if you "should" go to a friend's birthday party but parties really aren't your thing, you may realize that what you are getting from this is making your friend feel loved on her birthday. Well instead of the party you "can" take her to lunch or create a special present for her and let her know that you love her, but the party is not for you.

"Eliminate the Shoulds" is not a one-time exercise. It is something you can do every time you think you "should" do something you don't want to. Take your "Should" and turn it into a "Can".

Have the courage to pick your own unique direction.

When Your Direction is Terrifying

There will be some of you who are reading this book who feel that the risk of heading in the direction of their authentic self is too great. This is usually due to family and financial obligations. And this is a valid fear.

We have talked a few times about the fear of embarrassment and discomfort. And I hope that at this point all of you feel more equipped to deal with those fears.

But there are those of you who are truly dealing with fears of safety. The fear of not having enough food on the table or a roof over your head. And for you, my advice is to not give up on what you have discovered, but to make your fears work for you.

How do you make your fears work for you?

First, be sure that you are working to eliminate fears that are really just unhealthy beliefs. Fears of embarrassment, discomfort, and failure.

Then for those fears that are left, your real fears, like perhaps being sure that you make enough money to pay the rent on your family's apartment, embrace those as part of your authentic self. Make them part of your vision for your authentic self. Do not let them be something that you feel is going to hold you back from your dreams but make them part of your dream.

So, if you decided that making $600 or more a month is part of what makes you feel happy and successful then when you have an opportunity that sounds great but is unpaid, you pass it by because it does not align with your authentic self of bringing home enough money to pay the rent. Then continue on your journey of finding something that is in alignment with your entire authentic self, salary included. With this mindset you feel empowered to make decisions that are right for you instead of feeling like you have missed out on an opportunity because you can't take the risk.

Keeping a positive, abundant attitude, instead of a fearful one, about the direction you are taking, goes a long way in creating an exceptional life.

You get to make many choices along your journey. Have the courage to head in a direction that is in alignment with you.

15.

Life is a Web, Not a Ladder

"Each of us is a unique strand in the intricate web
of life and here to make a contribution."

– Deepak Chopra (New Age teacher)

Most of society views life as a ladder. Where there is one guy on
top and the rest of us are scrambling up the rungs trying to get to
that top spot. Where there is always someone above us who we are
trying to knock off and always someone below us who is trying to
pull us down.

Viewing our achievements as good, better, best keeps us small and
mediocre. It keeps us feeling like we are always lacking something,
that we always have to go higher.

To live the exceptional life that we want, we instead need to look
at life as a web.

There is No "Best"

From far back in history, when we lived in societies of tribes, we operated in a web. Groups of people shared a living space, and all worked together to keep the group alive. Some hunted, some foraged, others gathered. At times the hunters brought in the food. At other times it was the gatherers. Neither job was more important. Neither job was better.

Each role worked to the best of their ability to provide for the tribe. And everyone was grateful for the others in the tribe. There was no "mine" or "yours." Mostly because everyone supporting each other to do their best job meant less chance that they were all going to starve to death.

Can you imagine would have happened to humanity if the earliest people had decided the being a hunter was the most important job? Everyone fighting to be a hunter would leave a great lack of gatherers and in times that there was little game there would be no food from other sources. And we would have starved, and you and I wouldn't be having this conversation right now.

But somewhere along the way, we lost the sense that we all play an equal part in the success of humanity.

A few centuries ago, things changed. We moved into a landowner society and life became a ladder. "Ownership" became more important than community and making war over "ownership" became more important than protecting humanity. He with the most land, won.

Don't get me wrong, structure can be a good thing if it is used to organize, but this was used to suppress. There was one guy on top and someone under him and someone under him. There was a king and then barons and then tradesmen and the farmers and then slaves. Everyone's value was determined by where they stood on the ladder of ownership, so the goal was to have as many people as possible underneath you.

If you happened to be the most passionate and talented farmer, you were still under the tradesman and everyone else. So, you formed the belief that you did not want to be a farmer. That you wanted to "rise above" being a farmer. That you needed to send your kids to an apprenticeship to have a better life even if what they loved was being a farmer. It would be better to be a mediocre blacksmith than a great farmer because it was higher on the ladder.

In reality, this is where we still are today. There are some careers that are the top of the ladder and some that are at the bottom. And most of us spend our lives trying to claw our way up, forgetting our true selves and stepping on whoever we have to on the way.

But that is not our human nature. We are meant to connect with each other—with equity and quality—each bringing our unique gifts, our authentic selves. We are all different. None are better than another.

Let go of the belief that there is a ladder. Let go of the comparison. Let go of "the best." Embrace unique and essential.

Comparison is a Killer

When you view life as a ladder you are constantly comparing yourself to others. And comparing yourself to others is one of the easiest ways to feel bad about yourself.

When you view life as a ladder, you see everyone on social media as having a "better" time than you, you see people on TV as "better" looking than you, you see people at work as "more" wealthy than you, you see your neighbor as "more" accomplished than you. You see all of the people who are higher on the ladder than you.

And these negative comparisons make you feel inadequate, jealous, and inferior. Viewing life as a ladder steals your exceptional life from you.

When you view life as a web, you can see that the unique and special qualities you bring are not better or worse than anyone else's, only different. While that person over there may bring a higher IQ, you bring an out-of-the-box kind of creativity. While that person brings a classically good-looking face, you bring an inspired fashion sense.

If you live in the mindset that life is a web, you can never again feel like you are beneath anyone else and that, my friend, is what an exceptional life looks like.

When you are living your authentic life, you are more able to stop comparing yourself to others. Because you feel awesome and you don't need to judge your worth against others.

When I owned the bakery, I had that ladder mentality and was constantly comparing myself to others. I would look at other bakers' cakes and make comments in my head about what I did "better" instead of appreciating the differences or being inspired. In classes I took, I felt the need to be the "best" in the class and perhaps even show off a little instead of focusing on what I was learning. I even tanked an interview for Cupcake Wars because I was afraid I wouldn't be on the top of the ladder. When I was baking, I was never confident because I was not being myself. And I always found myself lacking compared to others.

Now that I have discovered my authentic self while writing this book and homeschooling my kids, I see life so much more like a web and I look to others for inspiration and collaboration. I am not concerned that there are people out there who will have books that rank higher than mine on Amazon because I know I am sharing unique and valuable information. I am not concerned with who might be "better" at homeschooling because I love the creative way I educate my children. I am confident and I don't need validation from anyone else. I look at everyone in my circle not as someone to surpass but as someone to learn from and collaborate with. And I find my life utterly abundant.

Appreciate what unique and special things you bring to the web. And appreciate what everyone else brings too. And leave it at that.

Be Part of a Web

The greatest leaders operate from the position that their teams are webs, not ladders.

There are plenty of high-achievers in leadership positions who have gotten where they are by stepping on the heads and backs of those in the way and by keeping them down. These are not leaders. Their power is an illusion, it is selfish and shallow and weak and cannot be maintained over the long haul. Their grip on the top rung is fragile. Eventually they will be pulled from the top rung by someone hungrier. Think Nero and Mussolini.

These people are not driven by their passion but by power.

But there are leaders who positively impact the world by inspiring and uplifting their teams. They view their team as a tribe made up of uniquely talented, equally important individuals. They help and support their tribe and do what they can to enrich each of their lives. They desire each member of the tribe to grow to their greatest potential because it is beneficial to the tribe. They know that supportive, vulnerable, healthy relationships are the foundation to everything they want to achieve.

These are individuals who know their authentic selves. They embrace their passion and fine tune their talents. They are clear on the impact they want to make and are living in their integrity. These are individuals who have aligned their lives with this and make no apologies. They live an exceptional life. And this sense of abundance allows them to encourage everyone else to do the same.

Take Google CEO, Sundar Pichai, who believes in collaboration, empowerment, and letting others succeed. He said, "it is less about trying to be a success (yourself) and more about making sure you have good people and your work is to remove that barrier, remove roadblocks for them so that they can be successful in what they do."

I encourage you to find yourself working with a leader who inspires and encourages you and not the guy on the top of a ladder.

Get Off the Ladder

There are plenty of places in your life where you are already part of a web. Places where you are excited to bring your authentic self to the table. Places where you are flourishing in the unique contribution of everyone.

But there are probably still areas in your life that you are viewing as more like a ladder. Areas where you are comparing yourself to others and trying to figure out how to climb higher.

VISUALIZATION: "Virtual Campfire"

Find a quiet place and sit down with your journal. You are going to take a deep look at the places in your life where you feel you are stuck on a ladder.

On a blank page in your journal, make two columns. In the first column, write down the names of ten people you are, well... jealous of. The people you think are on the ladder above you, stepping on your fingers. In the second column, write down what each of those people have that you don't. Money, awards, love, a 1972 Dodge Dart.

You will most likely see some themes. Pick the three areas of lack that repeated the most or that feel the most painful to you. With each of these three areas, we are going to do a visualization.

For each area where you feel you are lacking, I want you to imagine you are

---

sitting around a campfire with the people who have what you want, the people you are jealous of. I want you to imagine yourself feeling that lack.

Visualize yourself telling the others what you have been jealous of. Break the ice and watch what happens. Then I want you to listen as each of the people around the campfire tell you what they feel they are lacking and what they feel that you have, and they don't. You may not know these people very well and you may be thinking that you have no idea what they would say. Pretend! Fantasize! Let go! I promise you, what you hear them telling you in your imagination will be valuable. Don't overthink it, just give it time.

By the time the fire dies down, it will become apparent that you are not really on a ladder with these people, but in fact, in a web. Nobody around the campfire is any "better" than anyone else. We all have our strengths and our challenges. We are all different.

"Virtual Campfire" helps you to release the feeling that others are "better" than you and helps you let go of the areas in your life where you feel like you are desperately climbing a ladder.

In order to live an exceptional life, you must let go of the idea that there is a "best" or a top of the ladder. Embrace your unique authentic self and everyone else's.

16.

Make Fearless Choices

"In a choice between love and fear, choose love."

- Marianne Williamson (spiritual teacher)

Now that you know your authentic self and you are embracing the idea that it is essential to take the path that is in alignment with your authentic self, you might be wondering exactly how you do that daily.

Use Your Direction to Make Decisions

In your life, you will be faced with countless opportunities to choose from. Where to live. What to major in. Which job to take. Where to volunteer your time. So many decisions.

When you are deciding, I want you to learn to ask yourself, "Is this in alignment with my authentic self?" It is a simple yet powerful question that helps you make decisions in the direction of your greatest authentic self. Let me repeat, learn to ask yourself, "Is this in alignment with my authentic self?" If you don't ask, you end up making decisions that take you down a path that is not exceptional. I did that.

When I was deciding on colleges, I made a list to help me. A pro and con list.

I was choosing between University of Pennsylvania (Penn), Johns Hopkins, and Cornell and I really wasn't sure. Okay, I was sure. My gut said Penn. But I ignored it. (We'll talk about your intuition a little bit later, by the way.)

Anyway, I ignored my gut and I made a list. For each college, I had a column of what was good and a column of what was not so good. Average salary upon graduation, number of students in a class, access to professors, food, and so on. The list pointed me to Cornell and that is where I went.

The only problem was that I could not have cared less about what was on the list. Nothing on that list had anything to do with my authentic self. That list was a general comparison between schools but had nothing to do with me (it may have actually been my parent's list).

If I had thought about my authentic self I would have looked at having a single room (since I really liked my alone time), a great extracurricular dance program (because I didn't want to give it up even if I couldn't study it), proximity to a big city (that was a given), and a whole list of things that never made it on to my pro/con list.

I made a choice based on a list that was meant for someone else and ignored what was truly meant for me. I picked the option that looked "the best." Not realizing that "the best" is different for everyone.

If you decide to make a pro/con list for how your decisions align with your authentic self, and you find that none of your options align that well—don't be afraid to go out and look for other options. Don't rule anything out! Be creative. Don't dismiss what you know is right for you.

Bottom line, when you are making a decision, please don't compare the opportunity to criteria that everyone else thinks is important. Compare it only to your own authentic self. And be sure it fits to your liking.

Love vs Fear

Sometimes you are choosing between two options and often, you pick the safe one. Realize that when you are deciding between two options, you are really deciding between love and fear.

There is usually one choice that makes you so excited. It makes your heart race, it feels so right. But there may be something scary about that choice, so you look at the alternate choice that is really just quite a bit safer.

The first option is following what you love. The second option is running from what you fear.

This past summer my daughter had to decide between two options. She could spend the month of August as a trainee in a contemporary ballet company or she could hang out at home. She loved to dance. She loved the theater that the new ballet company is part of. She loved performing. She loved meeting new people. She loved the director. No brainer, right? But, there's a "but." She was afraid that she would not be good enough. So, she was undecided.

I asked if I could assure her that she would be good enough, which option would she choose. It was clear to her then. She was only considering staying home because she was afraid. But if she could be brave, she knew which option was built on love. When you remove the fear, everything becomes clear.

She spent the month in the trainee program and loved it so much that she is doing it again. She was glad and grateful she chose love over fear.

When I am choosing between things I am constantly asking "love or fear." I use it when I am picking an item off a menu and I am afraid I shouldn't get dessert or when I am considering canceling plans with a friend because I am tired or when I am buying a new couch with a crazy pattern. I choose love.

I don't let fear of discomfort or fear of others' beliefs or fear of embarrassment or fear of lack or fear of being taken advantage of keep me from what lights me up inside. I always choose love over these forms of fear. (I will admit that fears for health and safety get weighed differently. Health and safety boundaries are different for everyone and are something to be explored as part of your authentic self.)

When you look at your choices as one that draws you towards what you love, towards your authentic self, and one that protects you from something you fear, the choice becomes clear.

Choosing something that feels a bit scary is, well, pretty scary. But you know what's even scarier? Regret.
Let's try to avoid that, shall we?

Say "Yes" to Exceptional Opportunities

Even better than making decisions, let the decisions come to you.

Many times, you will be with decisions to make, but sometimes you will have an opportunity presented to you. Sometimes it will be something you jump at but other times it will be an opportunity that you don't think has anything to offer or might even be a little scary. But, by grabbing on to opportunities that the Universe presents to you, you are opening yourself up to finding a joyful, exceptional life that you might never have known was possible.

Leadership expert, Robin Sharma, said, "Keep believing that the Universe is a friendly place. The world really does want you to win. Let go of the control that most of us live the best years of our lives under and choose to be curious instead. You'll find that if you live this way, then a force more powerful than yourself will lead you to your best life on a daily basis."

What does Robin mean? He means that you need to embrace not only the opportunities that you think are great but those that you might have some doubts about. If they are in alignment with your authentic self, that is!

Be open.

The Art of Surrender

This art of surrender is covered wonderfully in *The Surrender Experiment* by Michael Singer. Michael conducted an experiment while he was in his twenties in pursuit of enlightenment. He decided to see what would happen if he stopped giving in to his personal fears and desires. He decided to surrender to whatever life had in store. His journey led him to living alone in the woods to becoming a computer programmer and finally a corporate CEO. By saying "yes" to the opportunities that were placed in front of him by the Universe, and that he had many doubts about, he created a thriving spiritual community, a transformative software package, a company whose achievements are archived in the Smithsonian, and a book that became a bestseller. All providing him with great joy.

After reading *The Surrender Experiment*, I decided to try it myself.

I was in the process of opening a small, custom bakery. On this particular day I was in the shop unpacking my tools and setting my space. I was not open for business.

There was a knock at the door. My preference was to not answer the door. I was busy and didn't want to be disturbed. But I had to say "yes" because of the experiment. I opened the door and in walked this elegant, dark-haired older woman who introduced herself as Suzanne. Suzanne waltzed in and sat right down on one of the chairs in my consultation area and started asking me all sorts of questions.

I, of course, wanted to brush her off because I was attending to what I thought was in my best interest, hurrying to get the place set up. But I said "yes" and sat down and engaged in answering her questions.

Suzanne then explained that she had a friend, a famous hair stylist in New York City, and she wanted a unique Christmas gift for him. Could I make a gingerbread house that looked like his salon, she wanted to know. "Well, no", I thought. "I'm not open yet and I make cakes, not gingerbread houses." But I said "yes". I took the job and made the gingerbread salon—which turned out to be a lot of fun by the way.

When Suzanne came to pick it up the following week, she was so delighted that she asked if I could make a snowman cake. In fact, a dozen for her friends! And oh, wait, how about ten dozen cookies for her holiday party. On top of her own orders, she sent many of her friends to me.

As a result of my letting go of my fears and personal desires, I opened the door figuratively (and literally) to a tremendous opportunity. Because of Suzanne I made a profit my very first month in business. What a blessing that I said "yes!"

We need to be open to learning the art of surrender and letting ourselves be guided by a force more powerful than us.

I encourage you to give it a try.

Experiment with Surrender

I want you to experiment with surrendering.

EXPERIMENT: "Say Yes"

For the next week, I want you to say "yes."

Say "yes" to any suggestion, opportunity, or activity that presents itself*.

Stop thinking about what could go wrong or how you should be doing something else or how much work it will be. Just say "yes."

Feel free to start small. Surrender to the things that are not super scary but really don't sound appealing to you. Like going to a concert you are drawn to or calling a friend who pops into your mind. (I surrender to flossing my teeth whenever I notice the dental floss.) Then work your way up to saying "yes" to things that make you a little more than nervous.

See what happens!

Write down these experiences in your journal. Note what you said "yes" to and note anything that happened as a result. Something good may happen or you may avoid something not so good. And it may not happen right away, but I can guarantee that one day you will be feeling really great about something and say "Wow, I sure am glad I said yes."

*Please note that you might find that you are presented with an opportunity that conflicts with something else you are already committed to doing. You have to make your own call here, but I tend to believe that you stick to your commitments. But you get to choose for yourself. Also, note that a suggestion, opportunity, or activity that clearly goes against your authentic self is not on the table for you. Being presented with the opportunity to get in the car with a drunk driver is not in alignment with your authentic self. Neither is stealing. Nor harming others. There is nothing to surrender to, these are not opportunities.

"Say Yes" is a practice I would love for you to incorporate into your life. Because the Universe really does know how to help you stay in alignment with your authentic self!

Surrender is a beautiful art to learn. It enables you to receive so much more than you ever imagined.

Dealing with the Doubt

Some opportunities might seem extra scary and we are really afraid to take them. Know that when we have trouble taking a certain opportunity (either through decision or surrender) it is because we are attached to gaining a particular result. We want things to work out the way we want them to!

We learned in a previous chapter that we can't be sure of how anything is going to work out, so that is not a valid reason to dismiss an opportunity.

I know. It can be hard to take that scary path, but I have a couple of ways to help your mind let go of the doubt about a decision.

It's Not a Risk, It's an Experiment

Often we are afraid that a decision will end in failure. And we pass on the opportunity even though it speaks to our authentic self.

We need to remind ourselves, for every opportunity, that "it's not a risk, it's an experiment." With that mindset, there is no possibility of failure!

The key here is to go into every opportunity with the mindset of a student. Your objective is to learn and to move forward on your journey. You have no idea how the opportunity is going to turn out, and with no expected result there can be no failure. There can only be learning. Sometimes you learn how to push humanity ahead with some great achievement and sometimes you learn what doesn't work and sometimes you acquire loads of self-knowledge.

If you go into every opportunity with an expectation, there are only two outcomes: success or failure. And that either/or mindset will cause a lot of people to pass over opportunities. Like asking someone on a date. Or auditioning for a role in the play. Or running for President. If your only options are success or failure, there is a good chance you just won't try. Because failure is not a comfortable outcome.

But if you enter in to any of those opportunities with no expectation you can only be surprised by learning something new.

I have repeated, "It's not a risk, it's an experiment," almost daily since I started writing this book. Because if I hold the expectation that writing this book is going to open the door to a whole new career for me and I am going to make millions and I am going to transform the lives of an entire generation, then I have a whole lot to fail at. But I hold in my mind that I am experiencing writing this book. I am going to do the best job I can and put my whole self into it and I am going to finish it. What happens after that? We'll see. It may be a bestseller, or it may open a different door for me or it may have only been a great learning experience. I am aligned with my authentic self, I am moving forward, I have no expectation.

There is no risk of failure.

Are you familiar with a quote by author Bryant McGill? "Everyone and everything is a teacher unless you are a poor student." It is a wonderful reminder to each of us that every opportunity holds growth for us. Everything moves us to a place we have not previously been. No moment is wasted. Nothing is a failure with this mindset. Everything is a successful lesson. Be eager to learn what life has to teach you.

When you come from the viewpoint of your decisions being experiments, it takes the pressure off. All you have to say is, "I am going to try this and see what happens." Then you are free to follow the opportunity without being attached to a particular result. Who can argue with that?

Really, What Could Happen?

I have just advised you to put your fears aside and let go of the need to have a safe, expected result from all of your decisions.

You have to be pretty brave to do that.

I have an exercise you can do when you are feeling a little less than courageous.

EXERCISE: "Worst Case Scenario"

When you are faced with a decision that your authentic self wants to make but the rest of you is doubting, I want you to grab your journal and make a list.

A list of the top ten worst case scenarios.

Say you are drawn to drop everything and backpack around the world for a year. Your worst case ideas might be running out of money and going hungry, not being able to get a job when you get back, making your parents mad, smelling funny. You get the idea.

Then I want you to look at each worst case and write about how you would handle it. It might be as simple as "suck it up" because when you look at your fear under the microscope it may be so manageable that you don't even have to handle it! Other scenarios might require you to do a few things alongside your great opportunity like setting up some small jobs on your trip or taking online classes during the journey. A few scenarios might really be something you don't think you can handle. I would then suggest talking them out with someone who might be able to help you find a way.

"Worst Case Scenario" helps you see that when you look at your fears closely, they may not be quite so scary.

Doubt can cast a huge shadow over your exceptional life, holding you back from opportunities that feel good to your soul. Learning how to manage your doubt goes a long way toward allowing you to make decisions that align with your authentic self.

Live an exceptional life by making decisions that propel you in the direction of your greatest authentic self.

17.

Embrace the Plot Twist

"Sometimes things fall apart so better things can
fall together."

- Marilyn Monroe (icon)

There are going to be moments when things don't go your way.
And you are having a hard time with the whole "surrender" thing.
There will be times when things actually seem pretty bleak and you
begin to lose faith in your ability to follow the desires of your
authentic self to lead an exceptional life.
When that happens, I want you to yell "plot twist" at the top of
your lungs.

Plot Twist

Plot Twist. Like in a book or a movie when everything is going great
but then it's not. Because there has been a plot twist. And you know
what? A plot twist is good.

Can you imagine how boring a book or movie would be if
everything worked out perfectly? And if you think about it, can you

imagine how boring life would be if everything worked out perfectly? If you knew exactly what was going to happen all the time? If you were never challenged intellectually or emotionally? Plot twists are what make our lives memorable! (Go watch the movie *Pleasantville* if you are not convinced that a completely perfect life isn't exactly joyful.)

Every once in a while, we need a plot twist. When we get off track from our authentic self. A plot twist tries to help us to make a change that puts us back on our best path. If we are open to these challenges they will help us to grow and create a better self.

Like in the book or movie. The plot twist makes our main character stop and take notice of what is not working in their story. And with that knowledge they can make some vital changes that actually propel them forward to that happy ending. And when you are done with the book you look back at that plot twist and think, "thank goodness that happened."

Actually yelling "plot twist" is a great way to snap yourself out of a potential downward spiral and remind yourself that sometimes your life needs a bit of shaking up.

Working with the Twist

When you look at not so great moments and reframe them as, "plot twists," you shock yourself out of panic and give yourself a chance to think clearly. You snap yourself out of negative thinking and doubt. You allow yourself to view the situation in a different light and begin to move forward.

There are even steps you can take to use the plot twist to your advantage.

Good Thing. Bad Thing. Who Knows.

You don't know how a situation is going to impact your life, so don't panic!

I am going to tell you my favorite story—ever. It is an ancient Sufi tale about an old man and his understanding that you don't know what anything is going to mean.

An old man lived in a beautiful valley with his son, a handsome and good youth. They lived a peaceful and happy life despite a lack of money and possessions and were very happy.

The old man used almost all of his savings to buy a young wild stallion. It was a beautiful horse and he planned to use it for breeding. The same night he bought it, it jumped over the fence to the paddock and disappeared into the wild. The old man's neighbors came over and commiserated, "How terrible," they said.

"Good thing? Bad thing? Who knows?" said the old man.

The next day, the stallion was back. And it brought a herd of about a dozen wild horses. The old man was able to lure all of them into his paddock, which he had fixed so escape was no longer possible. "What good fortune," said the neighbors as they clustered around.

"Good thing? Bad thing? Who knows?" said the old man.

His son started to train the horses. One of them knocked him down and stomped on his leg. It healed badly and left him with a permanent limp. "Such misfortune," said the neighbors.

"Good thing? Bad thing? Who knows?" said the old man.

The next summer, the King declared war. Soldiers came to the village and rounded up all the young men. The old man's son was spared because of his bad leg. "Truly you are lucky," exclaimed his neighbors as they bemoaned the losses of their sons.

"Good thing? Bad thing? Who knows?" said the old man.

And so, it went on forever.

The point of the story? Sometimes an event seems like a bad thing. But we don't know. It could in fact be a good thing.

They are really all just things. We are the ones who describe them as "good" or "bad".

My advice to you, when a plot twist happens, is to first remind yourself that you have no idea if this is a "good thing" or a "bad thing". Allow yourself to just let it be a "thing".

And then move on.

Don't Set Up Camp

It is human nature to feel bad when something doesn't go as you expected.

But what if you are having a hard time letting go of the notion that what has happened to you is a "bad thing?" When you were so attached to the situation turning out a different way that you don't even know what to do? What if you want to unpack all of your gear and set up camp? What if you want to fight against what is happening?

Many of us get stuck in toxic feelings of fear. We are so angry or jealous or sad or judgmental. We are still asking why this situation happened to us. We are wishing it would go away. We are getting ready to spend a great deal of time in this place of misery.

When you are that stuck, I encourage you to pull out your journal and analyze why you are feeling so badly, why whatever this is hit a nerve (resist the urge to judge yourself or this process).

PRACTICE: "Why?"

Ask yourself "Why am I feeling so afraid/angry/sad/jealous/judgmental?" Let the answer flow.

Then in response to that answer, ask yourself "Why?"

Respond and ask yourself "Why?" again.

Do this until you have asked "Why?" seven times. At that point you will most likely have gotten to the deeply held reason you are feeling so strongly about this situation.

Work on letting it go. Which is easier said than done. But I have faith that with some introspection, you can do it. It may not even be something that is a good idea to do on your own. Some traumas require gentle handling from a professional counselor or therapist and I encourage you to seek out help if that feels right to you.

"Why?" allows you to tap into your subconscious and see issues you did not even know you had. It really clears some blocks and allows you to move forward out of your feeling of despair and "why me".

Move Forward, Never Looking Back

When you get to the point of accepting the plot twist as just a "thing"—neither good nor bad—you are ready to move forward.

Look at this plot twist as a message from the Universe that the route you were heading on was not the one that was going to help you to become the greatest version of your authentic self. It was not leading you to an exceptional life.

When the path you thought you wanted to take is no longer available, you have the opportunity to start fresh and pick a new path. A path that is going to help you grow and lead you toward creating a better you.

There is a story about Ernest Hemingway and a gigantic plot twist.

In 1922, Hemingway was in Switzerland working as a correspondent for the Toronto Daily Star. A journalist there was impressed by young Ernest and asked to see more of his writings. Hemingway messaged his wife in Paris and asked her to bring his other work to Switzerland. She boarded a train the next day with a suitcase full of Ernest's writings. Everything she could find in the apartment. Everything he had been working on for who knows how long.

During a stop on the train, his wife got off to buy a bottle of water. When she returned, the suitcase was gone. At this point, Hemingway was unpublished and every word he had written, save one short story, was gone. His wife had even packed the copies!

Despite his loss, Hemingway recovered and in a few years, he went from being an unknown author to one of the most important writers of his generation. He produced some of the most important works of 20th century fiction like, *In Our Time*, *The Sun Also Rises*, and *A Farewell to Arms*.

Hemingway dealt with his feelings of sadness and anger, accepted the plot twist as just a "thing" and moved on in the direction of his authentic self. Hemingway said, "The world breaks everyone, and afterward, many are strong at the broken places." Words to live by.

I want you to think for a moment how Hemingway's life would have been different if his suitcase had never been stolen. Might he have been so involved with trying to sell those manuscripts that he would never have written his masterpieces? Perhaps. But it doesn't even matter. His story had a happy ending (this part at least) because he didn't get stuck in his despair and he used it to move forward to an exceptional place.

Moving forward is all about your attitude. An attitude of "opportunity." You have the opportunity to let go of the "why me" feelings. You have the opportunity to accept where you are right now. You have the opportunity to determine how you can be your very best self in this moment. This is the first step in recovering from a "failure," allowing you to move forward in a more positive, healthy direction. No good can come from living a past hurt over and over again. Once you have dealt with and even explored your pain, it is time to put it behind you. The experience will always be part of who you are, but don't let it hold you back from becoming who you are going to be.

It is difficult to find the story of someone who has achieved greatness who did not face some sort of adversity.

I bet you have a story.

The Silver Lining

I am sure that you have faced plot twists in your own life. Did you ever have your heart set on a college or a job only to be rejected? And after you had taken a different path did you realize that you were in the place you were meant to be? Did you maybe even thank your lucky stars that the other option didn't work out?

If you look back on your life at situations that you thought were "bad things," after you have had the gift of time, you can almost always see the silver lining.

Let's look together now.

EXERCISE: "Failure Map"

Grab your journal and a quiet spot.

I want you to list five of your greatest failures and disappointments. Your plot twists. Not getting in to the school of your choice. Not making a sports team. Your parents getting divorced. Getting dumped.

Then I want you to spend a few minutes with each one and I want you to

---

recognize what benefit those plot twists provided you. What did you do instead? What did you learn? How did you grow? Who did you meet?

Realize that those wonderful things may not have happened if not for your plot twist.

Save this page for yourself to refer back to whenever you meet a plot twist you don't think you can handle!

"Failure Map" helps you to remember how far you have come in life despite the plot twists that have been thrown at you. It reminds you that there is always a way forward.

When life gives you lemons, know that you can get calm, move forward, and make some lemonade, lemon meringue pie, lemon popsicles, and some vegan lemon soap. Take those lemons and make them your own.

You now have the tools to gracefully handle any plot twists that come your way. Maybe even with a smile.

18.

Don't Be Afraid to Change Direction

"Not all who wander are lost."

– J. R. R. Tolkien (author)

You Are Evolving

You are not making a decision and living with it forever. You are learning and experiencing life in alignment with your authentic self. And you are free to change your direction to stay in alignment.

As you live and grow and experience life, you will undoubtedly discover new things about yourself. You may uncover a new talent. Or you may become aware of a situation that tugs at your heart and drives you to make an impact. You may hit a dead end and realize that there are certain things that are not actually for you. You will always find new things that make you happy and characteristics you want to emulate. These discoveries may be tiny, or they may change the direction you are headed in.

What about that picture you drew of your authentic self? Tweak it every week! Update it once a month. Revisit all of the exercises once a year! This picture is a living document and is meant to evolve with you.

If you were honest when you were discovering your authentic self, you probably won't find the changes you encounter in the future to be that major.

However, if you had a lot of fears and limiting beliefs with you as you did the exercises, you may not have uncovered your deepest truths. If you spend time exploring yourself and shedding much of the negativity you carried, you may find that there are some significant changes. Don't be afraid. This is completely normal.

Side note. Have you ever heard of a mid-life crisis? When people pretty much throw away their current life for a new one? It is because people tend to enter a period of self-discovery around forty-two and they get in touch with their authentic self and are compelled to live in alignment with it. It happens to almost everybody and is nothing to be afraid of. I am hoping that the discovery you are doing now allows you to align your life with your authentic self now and not decades from now!

Look, setting a direction for your life that is aligned with your authentic self is a journey. It takes time and patience and effort to live an exceptional life. It is a winding path not a straight shot along the expressway.

Nothing is Wasted

Sometimes we realize we are off course. But don't despair, it is all part of your adventure. Everything you experience is valuable. Changing direction is not losing anything!

Change your major. Change your job. Change your life. You will still be taking everything you learned with you.

I know it is difficult and scary. To have put your blood, sweat and tears into something and then to realize that it is not the right direction for you. To have invested in a business or a college career or a relationship and come to know that it is not in alignment with your authentic self.

You can choose to suffer for a lifetime by sticking to a direction that is not yours or you can endure the quick pain of change. The choice is yours. It is painful either way. But only one lasts for a lifetime.

When you have put your everything into something you are not leaving empty handed. You are taking with you your skills and experiences that are an asset elsewhere. Even if you are leaving the path of an engineer and headed in the direction of an artist. You have learned skills in organization and planning and creativity. You have learned how things work and impact each other. You have learned various technologies.

Instead of looking at the art skills you lack and the engineering skills you will no longer be using, look at the skills you have acquired that can be transferred. Remind yourself of what you are bringing with you, not what you are leaving behind. You can even write your resumé based on those skills.

When I left my corporate career to open a bakery I thought I would be throwing away years of experience. But I brought with me the technology skills that allowed me to create my own website, inventory management system, and online ordering system. I used my engineering background to create the internal structures needed to create six-foot-tall Eiffel Tower cakes and cakes of the Miami Hurricanes Ibis mascot with a huge beak and skinny legs. And the customer service skills I had built over the years were essential in dealing with clients.

Just because I wasn't working in the exact same capacity did not mean that I was not making great use of my skills.

Every moment of your life changes you and allows you to grow in some wonderful way. Be aware of it and you will see that nothing is wasted.

Try New Things

It is incredibly important to try new things, all the time, if you want to live an exceptional life.

Trying something different, no matter what it is, is what helps you discover more about yourself.

Travel. Classes. Books. Skydiving. Romances. Volunteer efforts. A brand-new outfit. A different flavor of coffee. It doesn't matter what it is. Everything you do gives you more insight into who you are and what lights you up inside.

Think back to the chapter on surrender and say "yes" to opportunities that cross your path (unless you know that they go against your authentic self). Try that new food on your plate. Take that weekend getaway with your friend. Buy that sweater that drew your attention from across the store. Say "yes" to what life puts in your path and see how it feels deep inside yourself. Then incorporate what feels right into your vision of your authentic self.

Aside from learning more about yourself, trying new things has a few additional benefits.

Trying new things:

• helps you learn to overcome fear

- gives you interesting things to talk about
- stimulates creativity
- opens up new opportunities
- helps you meet new people
- makes you more marketable
- boosts your confidence
- teaches you patience

Make a habit of trying new things. It's good for you.

Life is meant to be lived. Follow your authentic self and try new things to discover new parts of yourself. And when you do something, and you decide it does not align with your authentic self, don't be afraid to move on.   There are no mistakes for everything you experience is of value.

So, change direction.   It is the only path to an exceptional life.

19.

Know That Education is Not One-Size-Fits-All

"You are the effort and expression, not the outcome."

- Bryant McGill (thought leader)

If you are at a point in your life that still involves school, I want you to explore education with me for a bit. Remember those misguided beliefs? You may have a few about education.

Education is About Learning

The best piece of advice that I can give someone about education is that education is not a prerequisite to something like a job or college, it is a learning experience. It is not a place to take the right classes and get the right grades in order to be awarded something you want. Education is about learning.

My oldest daughter is about to be a freshman in high school.

(Yikes!) Since she is homeschooled that means that I need to get a little bit on the ball about college. Because I want to understand the requirements for homeschoolers and be sure that I am tracking and recording and planning in a way that provides her with all of the "stuff" she will want to have to apply.

We started researching some colleges that she might be interested in (art program, small school, not too far away) and browsed around majors and courses and requirements. At some schools, we found majors so perfect for her that she bookmarked them for the future. At other schools, she loved the environment and thought she would love living there but then the courses that were required were simply not things that would excite her.

I am thrilled at the thought that in a couple of years she gets to browse through all this stuff for real. So excited that she will get to figure out what she is excited to learn about and where she will want to do that. I can't wait for her to continue to learn about what sets her soul on fire.

But then I had dinner with a few friends who have kids heading off to college. And their excitement about college for their kids was entirely different. It was about what job did they want to have four years from now and which college would hand them a diploma that was be the fastest ticket to that job. The only excitement was about the campus and the sports teams and the sororities. There was not one mention of being excited about what they would learn.

And that made me sad.

Because that is how I had approached college. Not as a learning experience but as a stepping stone to a job. And I can't say that I learned a lot while I was at college because I was not sitting in each class treating it as the educational experience it was meant to be but as a grade I needed to achieve. I left college with a diploma and little knowledge.

It is one of my few regrets in life. (But if that had not been my path, I would not be here today trying to help a whole new generation to take a different route. Plot twist!)

Education is meant to be about learning. It is about growing and questioning and exploring. It is about becoming a lover of learning and keeping that love throughout your life.

The greatest minds do not stop learning once they are handed a diploma. People like Elon Musk, Quentin Tarentino, Frank Lloyd Wright, Florence Nightingale, Walt Disney, Thomas Edison, Henry David Thoreau, Nelson Mandela, Elizabeth Barrett Browning, and Ansel Adams are a few examples of lifelong learners.

They didn't go to school to check a list of courses off their to-do lists. They went to school because they were curious and wanted to learn about things that interested them from people who were more experienced than they were. They are or were constantly seeking knowledge through experiences and mentors and books and classes. They were curious and asked questions and sought answers. They did not learn something as a means to an end, the learning was always the goal. And what they learned they incorporated into their being and carried them along to the next great question or discovery.

If you think back through most of history until about a hundred years ago, scholars wanted to be, well, scholars. They were not going to school to get a job. They were going to school to philosophize and debate and discuss. They went to school to be surrounded by other people who wanted to do the same. They wanted to experiment and write about what they found out and teach it to others. There was no reason to be there other than to learn.

I want every young adult to remember that the goal of education is learning. Learning about what lights their soul on fire. Changing their being through learning.

I want every young adult to let go of the thought that education is about a test result, a grade, and a diploma. To let go of the idea that they learn what they need to get an "A" and then let the knowledge go. Because it doesn't change them. It doesn't touch them. I want them to let go of learning because they have to, not because they want to.

My greatest hope for every young adult is that they change their beliefs about education.

That they stop looking at education as a means to an end. That they start looking at education as an opportunity to learn about what you love from the very best and with the very best. That they see education as a way to change their being. That they seek to learn long after their formal education is over.

My greatest hope is for a generation of lifelong learners.

Learning Happens in All Different Places

I'm just going to say it straight out.

College is not everything and it is not for everyone.

I believe that college is one option for education. There are jobs and apprenticeships and trade school and travel. And probably a dozen things I have not even dreamed about.

Again, you need to find a method of education that fits you. It may be a particular type of school or it may be something else entirely.

There is a modern obsession with the idea that every kid must go to college. As a society we have a belief that you need a college degree in order to make anything out of yourself. But it isn't true. Did you know that some of the best companies in the world no longer require a college degree to work for them? Among them are Google, Apple, Random House, and IBM.

Not every person is wired for academia and for those people, going to college is in direct conflict with their authentic self.

And that is utterly draining on the soul.

But they do it anyway because they feel that they need to follow the same path as everyone else.

But college should not be the go-to step after high school. It should be the place where you go to learn, remember?

My niece was brave enough to know that college was not for her. She wasn't clear on her passion or talents yet, so she took a year and joined AmeriCorps, a community service organization. She had many assignments throughout the United States and her final one was working with the forestry department fighting wildfires in Colorado. And she fell in love. She comes from a long line of firefighters and the experience reminded her that this was her passion. As her AmeriCorps service comes to an end, she is applying to become a Wildland Firefighter with the US Forestry Service.

I am so happy for her that she is following her own unique direction and embracing her authentic self.

I encourage you to look at college as only one of many options available to you. Not the only or best option. I encourage you to hold your vision for your authentic self and pick a direction that is in alignment with that.

It may be college. It may be taking classes that interest you and working. It may be an apprenticeship. It may be a gap year. It may be a career. It may be a volunteer opportunity. It may be starting your own business. And don't forget about books and people and travel. Look at every moment as a growth opportunity.

College may be exactly the right thing for you. Or it may not be.

Look at all the options. Think outside the box. Talk to people and ask lots of questions to truly understand what each option has to offer. Then look at how the options align with your authentic self. And have the courage to pick the direction that is yours.

Decide on an advanced education that is uniquely yours so that you can start living your exceptional life now.

20.

Do Away with Resistance

"When you really get where people are coming from,
they are far more likely to let you take them where
you want to go."

– Unknown

At this point, I bet you are excited that you know yourself and
that you are preparing to align your life with your authentic self and
follow your own unique direction.
Your parents, however, might not be as enthusiastic as you are.
Let's explore what is going on with your parents a bit more so that
you can talk to them about your direction in a way that will make
them listen.

Inside the Mind of a Parent

Remember how we talked about your parent's fear of embarrassment
and pain earlier in the book?
Let's dig a little deeper.

Your Parents Are Wired to Keep You Safe

Your parents love you and everything they do is because they love you. Keep this in mind. Please.

Your parents want you to be happy. But more than that, they want you to stay alive and succeed. It dominates their thinking. It is their natural instinct.

Back in the olden days, a parent's main concern was what they had to do to keep their child from being eaten by a lion. Today they don't want you to end up dying in a gutter from a drug overdose or because of a bullying social media post or from jumping off a bridge because your friends all do it or traveling to a war-torn country. They also don't want you to have to live in a dangerous apartment or starve to death.

But different parents have different fears about safety.

I realized this when my oldest daughter was six months old.

I had two close friends with daughters the same age. Our kids grew up together and I had the opportunity to observe how we all viewed "safety" differently.

I was all about sleep. My daughter had to be home by two every afternoon for a nap. Otherwise she either would not nap at all and be a terror or she would nap too late and be up well past bedtime and then I would be a terror. I was always concerned about her sleep.

My friend, Iris, was concerned about food. While I gave my daughter healthy food at every meal, I did not concern myself if she ate. I knew she would eat when she was hungry. I never stressed out about it. But Iris played that, "here comes the choo-choo" game with every bite and made Sophia sit in her high chair until she had eaten everything. She was afraid Sophia would wither into nothingness.

And then there was my friend, Casey. She was concerned about staying warm. Little Randy always had to be bundled up. Even if the poor thing was clawing her clothes off. Casey was petrified that Randy would catch a cold from being free of her coat, scarf, and hat. I always dressed my daughter for the weather, but then let her choose if she was too warm. I never stressed out about that either. I didn't think she would die from hypothermia at the playground.

I didn't care about food or clothing, but oh sleep. I thought that was going to be the death of my darling baby! While Iris and Casey looked at me like I had two heads when we left every fabulous playdate early to get home for naptime and that I always had a book in the car in case I had to occupy myself if my daughter fell asleep before we got home. I can laugh about it today, but back then sleep felt like a real safety issue!

But isn't it funny how three parents can each have their own fears about safety?

Even today my fears are different from other parents I know. I am afraid of my kids traveling alone because of plane crashes while another is afraid of kidnapping and another of food poisoning in a foreign country!

And I bet your parents have their own safety concerns and they are different from the ones your friend's parents have. And they are certainly different from the ones you have.

Remember your parents love for you. Try to respect their fears, okay? Even if they seem ridiculous to you.

Feel the Love. And the Fear.

I don't want to utter the phrase, "you'll understand when you're a parent", so I am going to guide you through a little exercise that can help you put yourself in their place emotionally.

VISUALIZATION: "Lovey"

Take out your journal and find a quiet place.

I want you to pick the thing you love most in the world. Your pet. Your sister or brother. Your parent. Your best friend. Mr. Toad, your childhood stuffed animal.

Spend a few minutes thinking all sorts of wonderful thoughts about your lovey. I want you to get into how you feel when you are with them. Write down some of your emotions. Really feel the love.

Now I want you to do something difficult. Picture that your lovey is gone. That your lovey has died or is lost or is destroyed. Imagine your life without them. You won't have to ponder this too long because the emotions will flow right up. The fear, the sadness, the grief. Write it all down.

Keep this "Lovey" page handy. Refer to it whenever your parents are against your plans to remind yourself how they might be feeling.

Having a better understanding of what you parents are thinking can be a real asset in keeping an open mind about their reactions when you are talking to them.

Talk It Out

You have an understanding of your authentic self. You have an understanding of the fears that could be going on inside your parent's heads. You might be ready to talk to your parents about the direction you want to head in.

I have some suggestions for how to do that gracefully and peacefully.

Nothing Inspires Confidence Like a Well Thought Out Plan

The thing that gets parents to listen is when you are calm and clear about your needs. When you can explain yourself to your parents in a way that makes them realize that you have actually thought this through and are not just being random.

You have a crystal-clear picture of your authentic self. Share that with them.

You have done a lot of work to get to the point of knowing your authentic self. Explain how you got there. Describe the exercises and some of your important discoveries. I am not suggesting you have to give them your journal for some bedtime reading but share what you have learned.

Clearly sharing your plan with your parents shows them your maturity, thoroughness, and determination.

Showing them results is another great way to show them. Making your plan a reality before you talk to your parents can go a long way.

PLAN AND ACT: "A Picture is Worth a Thousand Words"

This exercise takes some planning and some execution over the course of a few weeks or months.

Grab your journal and brainstorm a page full of actions you can take that are aligned with your authentic self. These can be books you can read or classes you can take or part time jobs, an internship or volunteer opportunities or experiences or anything you can think of that will help you to grow your authentic self.

Pick your five favorites.

Create an action plan. What can you do today towards your action? This week? This month? Schedule these action items into your calendar.

Then get to work. Tackle your action items with great enthusiasm. You are starting your exceptional life. Right now.

Make some space in your journal to record what you are doing and what you are accomplishing. You can use this to show your parents that you are already working in the direction you want to head (and the bonus is that you are already working in that direction).

"A Picture Is Worth a Thousand Words" is a great way to illustrate your clarity and determination to your parents—and yourself

The Art of Conversation

When you talk to your parents about the direction you are going to head in, you may be sharing your decision with them or you may be seeking their agreement about your decision. Either way, you want the conversation to be peaceful and productive.

Here are a few suggestions.

- Know what you want. Do you want them to approve of your choice? Do you want them to agree to your choice? Do you just want to inform them of your choice? Do you want their opinion?
- Know your information. Be clear on your authentic self and the process you went through to discover it.
- Pick a good time. Pick a time when you parents are relaxed and not involved with a number of other things. Depending on your and your parents' personalities, it might be good to ask for a meeting or it might be better to be a little more impromptu.
- Be honest.
- Listen. Your parents have both valid concerns and vast experience. Listen to them and reflect on what you hear.

You might just learn something useful.
- Don't yell or argue. Ask to continue the conversation at another time if it becomes too heated.
- Ask for acceptance.

There is the possibility that you will not find common ground with your parents. In that case, I suggest finding another adult to talk to. A teacher, a friend, a religious leader, a coach, or a guidance counselor can be a great sounding board and help you to figure out how to continue talking to your parents or they can support you in living with the conflict.

Understand that if someone is not ready to hear something, they are going to be difficult to talk to. All you can control is what you say to them, not their reaction to what you say. Approaching the conversation with a well thought out plan and a desire to listen as well as be heard will do a whole lot towards you being understood.

Agree to Disagree

Even after having some heartfelt discussion with your parents, you may find that you simply cannot agree on the direction your life is going to go in.

You may choose to keep having discussions. You may choose or be required to go in the direction they prefer because you are a minor. You may choose to go in your own direction and continue to try to get them to embrace it.

Whichever direction you choose, I encourage you to approach it with tolerance.

Practice Tolerance

We have already touched upon how parents are trying to save themselves from the potential embarrassment that can be caused by your decisions. Realize that this is a real emotional issue for some parents.

Everyone in the world has beliefs about how the world works and what is "good" and what is "bad." Your parents included. These are beliefs that they have probably held since before you were born. These beliefs are part of your parents. Beliefs about religion and marriage and sexuality and education and lifestyle. Beliefs about clothing and food and friends. Beliefs about everything in life.

You have beliefs too. And sometimes they will conflict with those of your parents. And for most parents, your conflicting belief causes them embarrassment. Your nose piercing or your haircut or your boyfriend. Your choice of major or your apartment or your salary. These all have the potential for embarrassment if they conflict with your parent's beliefs.

Some parents are tolerant of their kids' alternative beliefs. They are secure enough in themselves to not see their child as a reflection of themselves. Even if they do not agree with your choices.

But there are many parents who are not that tolerant. However, nobody has ever died from embarrassment. Being afraid of being embarrassed by your decisions is something your parents need to tackle on their own.

But just as you wish for your parents to accept, or at least be open and tolerant to your beliefs, I encourage you to be open and tolerant to theirs. It can be scary for them to consider a way of life different from their deeply held beliefs.

"Your children are not your children. They are the sons and daughters of Life's longing for itself." I want to look up and read the beautiful poem, *On Children*, by Kahlil Gibran.

You might want to share this poem with your parents to help them to be more tolerant of your beliefs. To help them consider that you are on this earth to become your own person. And while they can support you and inspire you, they cannot command you. At least not forever.

We Are All the Same

You may end your discussions with your parents behaving in a way that you judge to be "bad" or "wrong." You cannot change your parents' behavior, but to live an exceptional life you must learn to find peace in this conflict.

PRACTICE: "I Am That"

This exercise comes from Conversations with God author, Neale Donald Walsh.

It is an exercise you can train yourself to do in every moment of every day, with everyone you meet.

The exercise is quite simple.

In every interaction you have, realize that you are making a judgement about the other person. And say to yourself, "I am that." It is really helpful to realize that you have, at some point in your life, behaved in a similar way as the other person. And that you are not "bad" or "wrong."

When someone rushes past you and bumps into you without an apology and you are judging them as rude, say "I am that" and realize that you too in your life have been preoccupied with your own thoughts and may have neglected being as polite as you could be.

When someone lies to you and you judge them as untrustworthy, say to yourself "I am that" and realize that you too in your life have lied, even a small lie.

When your parents react negatively to something you wish to do, and you judge them as mean or nervous or uncompromising, say "I am that" and realize that you have also been mean to someone or nervous about something or uncompromising in your own beliefs.

You have the opportunity to put yourself fully in someone else's shoes, even your parents. You have been provided with a different perspective which brings about acceptance and tolerance and peace.

"I Am That" is a life-changing exercise in tolerance and I hope that you make it a daily practice, with your parents and with everyone you encounter.

Your parents' fear of pain or embarrassment does not mean giving up on your beliefs or changing the direction of your life. It means giving the same tolerance and respect that you wish to be given by them.

Hopefully your parents will be as excited about your discovery and path as you are, but there is the chance that you may never get your parents to agree to the direction you want to take in life. But you can always treat their concerns with love, tolerance, and clear communication.

PART V

LIVE AN EXCEPTIONAL LIFE

You have discovered your authentic self and
have learned how to set a direction to live
your life in alignment with it. The final
step to living an exceptional life is to
surround yourself with the support
necessary to stay on your path.

21.

Be Grateful

"Life is a series of thousands of tiny miracles.
Notice them."

- Mike Greenberg (author)

Cultivating gratitude might be the easiest way to live an
exceptional life.
When you express gratitude, you are focusing your entire being
on the beautiful things you have instead of focusing on what you
might think you lack. Gratitude is the ability to express
thankfulness and appreciation for what you have. It is the ability to
look at what is going on in the present instead of longing for
something from the past or wishing for something in the future.
People who look at life with a sense of gratitude are always aware
of the terrific things in their lives—no matter how big or small these
things may seem. And when they encounter a plot twist, people
who are constantly grateful can easily put it into perspective.

Gratitude makes your life better in so many other ways too.
Gratitude has been proven to:
– create a feeling of greater happiness and optimism

– increase self-esteem

-heighten energy

-strengthen immune system and lower blood pressure

-improve intelligence

-expand capacity for forgiveness

-decrease anxiety and depression

-raise spirituality

There is no better way to live an exceptional life than to look at each moment and see it as exceptional.

PRACTICE: "Gratitude Journal"

Working toward living in gratitude is a wonderful daily practice. Try using a journal to help you form the habit.

Get a new journal and keep it next to your bed.

Every night before you turn in, make an entry in your journal listing three things that you are grateful for that day. They can be huge things like a project well done or little things like seeing a beautiful butterfly.

After you are in the habit, I encourage you to expand your practice of gratitude outside of your journal.

Set a bell on your phone and when you hear it, stop and note what you are grateful for.

In a tense situation, stop and think of three things you are thankful for about your current situation. This is great because it is difficult to be negative and positive at the same time!

READING LIST: "The Book of Joy"

To get a sense of the power of gratitude, I highly suggest *The Book of Joy* by Douglas Carlton Abrams. Abrams recorded a meeting between the Dalai Lama and Desmond Tutu during a birthday celebration for the Dalai Lama.

Both men are spiritual leaders for countries that have been torn apart by political and cultural unrest. Each has had many experiences that one would imagine would leave them in states of fear, anger, and sadness. But not these two.

Both men have cultivated such gratitude for their lives and their work that they are not only tolerant or accepting, they are joyful. I found myself in tears of joy throughout the book over how full the human heart can be. I encourage you to laugh and cry along with them during their short visit and experience this beautiful reminder that we can all be thankful and full of love, no matter what.

Feeling grateful for all that you have is what an exceptional life is really all about so make it an integral part of your life.

22.

Listen to Yourself

"Courage is being yourself every day in a world
that tells you to be somebody else."

– Unknown

So much of what we have covered in this book was about
listening to yourself. Don't stop now! In order to live an
exceptional life, you must constantly listen to your inner guidance,
so you are aware of how you might be changing and growing and
what opportunities might present themselves.

While it is wonderful to learn from others, you truly learn the
most from yourself. So, you would be wise to set aside time each
day to listen to your own wisdom.

I get up early each morning, well before the rest of the house, and
I grab a cup of tea and tiptoe up to a little room I made for myself
out of a closet on the third floor of my house. In the summer the
window is open, and I am eye-to-eye with the birds in the trees and
in the winter, I am snuggled under a blanket with a cat on my feet
while I wait for the heat to come on. But every day I am up there.

And I sit for about thirty minutes.

I start simply by closing my eyes and breathing. Then I immerse myself in one of the practices I will share with you in a bit. It differs each morning depending on my level of focus or if I am working on a particular problem or just listening.

Having this relaxed time each day has provided me with lots of new ideas. It has helped me work through issues that seemed overwhelming. The time has helped me focus on what's important to me and helped me to let go of situations and people that weren't good for me. It has inspired my creativity. And it has provided me with much greater peace and serenity in my life.

Clearing the chatter that is constantly filling your head allows you to listen to your inner self. Here are a few of the ways that I do that.

PRACTICE: "Quiet Time"

I cannot speak highly enough about the practice of meditation for getting in touch with your inner self. But you do not need to have a formal meditation practice, if that does not speak to you. Finding a few quiet moments with yourself each day is a fine form of meditation.

Decide on a time of day and pick a quiet place. I would suggest bringing your journal in case you want to record any of your insights.

Then each day, sit quietly, breathe slowly and deeply. You might want to put on some soft music, and then listen to your thoughts. Maybe record a few insights in your journal.

Start with five minutes.

That's all.

Once you fall in love with this practice, try doing it more than once a day. I have traded the habit of picking up my phone when I have five minutes to spare and instead close my eyes and listen.

PRACTICE: "Guided Meditation"

Being guided through a meditation is a great way to help focus your mind.

You are not actively listening to yourself, but you are training your mind to relax and get quiet which is necessary to listening.

There are plenty of videos on YouTube or apps you can download.

My favorite is the free *Insight Timer* app. You can just set a timer or play music, but you can also select from thousands of guided meditations on all topics and of varying lengths. There are also educational talks, courses, and a social support network.

READING LIST: "The Artist's Way"

While *The Artist's Way* by Julia Cameron is advertised as a book to get in touch with your creative self, I like to look at it as a way to get in touch with your deepest self.

The book guides you on a twelve week journey of discovery and arms you with two of the most powerful tools I have ever encountered for becoming more in tune with myself: "Morning Pages" and "The Artists' Date". Not only is this book a powerful tool, it is lots of fun!

While I highly suggest reading the book yourself, I have to at least tell you about "Morning Pages" and hope you incorporate them into your life.

"Morning Pages" is pulling out your journal every morning and simply writing. Just a dump of what's in your mind. No thinking or editing or judging, simply letting it all out. It is so freeing and revealing. A great way to hear what your inner self is trying to tell you. Three pages goes quickly if you are writing everything that pops into your mind!

Throughout this book you have done an outstanding job of listening to yourself. Keep it up in order to keep up your exceptional life.

23.

Find Your Tribe

"You show me your friends, I'll show you your future."

-John Wooden (basketball player and coach)

Living an exceptional if so easy if you have a tribe with you. When you surround yourself with people who are also striving to be their authentic selves and live exceptional lives, you see that your vision is possible and normal. You develop the courage to take the path less traveled and take your own unique direction because you see so many others doing it. You have a group to rely on when you hit bumps in the road instead of trying to figure them all out on your own. You have a cheering section. You have people who understand you and your drive. You have a tribe.

Finding your tribe is fairly easy once you discover your authentic self. Look to people who share your passion and want to grow the same or similar talents. Find groups that want to make the impact you want to make or who strive for the same ideas of success as you do. Team up with people who find happiness in the same ways you do. Find more than one tribe! Love them all!

You may have to build a tribe, person by person. Or you may find a group that easily becomes your tribe. Once you find your tribe, make a commitment to them and invest your time and energy. Do things together. Reach out to members when you need them for support. Be available when another tribe member needs you. Tell your tribe about your projects and let them hold you accountable. Tap your tribe when you need knowledge or motivation.

I have three important tribes in my life right now (and a few others as well).

I am part of a huge organization, called Mindvalley, which offers self-development courses and creates its own tribes on Facebook and at in-person events. These are people that I tap into when I am struggling with a problem or a new philosophy. I am there to provide my insights into their issues. We all take classes together online and help each other with the material. We share our successes and our struggles. Both online and in person.

I also have two close friends who are my tribe here at home. We all share a passion for education and for the spiritual side of life and for living a simple, natural life. We get together for breakfast once a month and share whatever is going on in our lives. We travel together once a year. And we text almost daily with book recommendations or blog posts that the others might enjoy.

Lastly, I have a tribe of one who supported me in writing this book. The tribe started out as forty writers but the connection I made was with this one woman in the United Kingdom. Our books are similar and through many conversations I learned that we share a lot of similarities when it comes to parenting and life philosophy. She has been a rock in this process of writing.

Finding your tribe is not hard if you know where to look.

ACTION: "Find Your Tribe"

To find your tribe, go out and try new things that are aligned with your
authentic self and talk to the people there.

-Take a class or workshop.

-Volunteer.

-Find a group online.

-Go to a meeting or conference.

-Attend an event.

-Form a club.

And chat! Ask lots of questions and find out about the people you meet.
When you meet someone you are really drawn to, arrange to meet again. For
coffee or at another event.

An exceptional life cannot be lived alone. Find
your tribe and find so many opportunities for
growth and sharing and joy!

24.

Seek Out a Mentor

"Alice: This is impossible. Mad Hatter: Only if you
believe it is."

- Lewis Carroll (author)

Throughout your exceptional life, you will always be a student.
Having an exceptional teacher is a must!
A mentor is someone who will support your authentic self and
help guide you along your journey. A mentor may be part of your
tribe and share some of your passions or talents—but they don't
have to. The only criteria for a good mentor is that they have a
passion for YOU.

A mentor will help you to be exceptional.
-They will listen without judgement.
-They can provide information and knowledge.
-They will support your experiments.
-They can ask questions that you might not have thought of.
-They will help pick you up and brush you off when you stray
from your path.
-They can point out areas for improvement.

-They can suggest ways to stimulate your growth.

-They can be sounding boards.

-They can play Devil's Advocate.

-They can connect you to others who can make a valuable impact on your life.

-They can share their experiences with you.

-They can serve as a role model.

-They will give you a push when you stop waking.

-They are free (but are priceless)!

ACTIVITY: "Ten People"

In picking a mentor, I suggest picking someone that you would be willing to trade lives with. Not necessarily what they have or do, but who they are. They should be a person whose character aligns with yours. They should be a person who is living their authentic self.

Before looking for a mentor, be clear on what you want out of a mentor. Are you looking for guidance on a particular project? Do you have a few questions that you want to have answered? Do you want to observe a successful person in the field you want to pursue? Do you want a general mentor? Be clear on what you are going to ask a mentor to do.

To find a mentor, make a list of ten people you admire. (You might actually want to look back to your notes on success!) Be sure that they are living their authentic life and that you would be willing to trade with them. Rank the remaining ones in order of preference.

Then... talk to them. Your favorite first. Tell them about your authentic self and your desire to have them as a mentor. Tell them what you would like out of the relationship and how long and often you would like to meet.

Go through your list of potential mentors until you find a match.

Be sure to send a thank-you note to anyone you talked to or who responded to your inquiry but was unable to be your mentor.

If there is no one in your life that you would consider as a mentor, explore

---

some online mentoring options. Try: *Ten Thousand Coffees*, *Coach.me*, *The Muse*, and *Meetups*.

When you have a mentor relationship, set up some time to regularly talk about what is going on in your life. Be prepared with questions. Be prepared to listen. Consider any suggestions your mentor provides. Read any books or take any courses they suggest. Keep them up to date on your progress and of the impact they are having on you and then, meet again.

A mentor can be so valuable in helping you move effortlessly along your journey.

PART VI

AND NOW ...

... you have completed a life-changing journey.

First, you opened your eyes to the message you are getting about what you should be doing with your life. You let go of the doubt about being able to make your own choices. You released the idea that you need to follow the same path as everyone else. You learned that being mediocre is no way to live. And you threw away the idea that life has to be hard.

With this newly opened mind, you discovered who you truly are. You remembered your passion. You embraced your talents. You uncovered the impact you want to make on the world. You learned what kind of person you want to be. And you clarified what makes you happy. You discovered your authentic self and committed to reminding yourself who you truly are, every day. This in and of itself is a noteworthy and incredible achievement!

Then you learned how to live each day moving in a direction that is in alignment with your authentic self. You considered the idea that what you are doing in each moment is important and that "best" is not what it's all about. You gained insight into how to make decisions, how to accept opportunities, and how to let go of expectations. You prepared for change. You explored what education is all about. And you readied yourself to have heartfelt conversations with the people who are concerned about you.

You considered some methods for living an exceptional life. Expressing gratitude. Listening to yourself. Finding your tribe and your mentor.

You are now armed with the knowledge and tools to live an exceptional life.

I encourage you to set up a practice in your life that allows you to check in with the vision you created of your authentic self, every day and when you have decisions to make.

And I encourage you to continue learning about methods for aligning your direction with your authentic self and for living an exceptional life.

Never stop striving to be more exceptional and joyful than you were the day before.

Made in the USA
Lexington, KY
03 June 2019